a***hole·ol·o·gy

a**·hole·ol·o·gy

Steven B. Green, Dennis Lavalle, and Chris Illuminati

AVON, MASSACHUSETTS

Published by
Adams Media, a division of F+W Media, Inc.
57 Littlefield Street, Avon, MA 02322. U.S.A.
www.adamsmedia.com

ISBN 10: 1-59869-910-5
ISBN 13: 978-1-59869-910-4

Printed in the United States of America.

10   9   8   7   6   5   4

Library of Congress Cataloging-in-Publication Data
is available from the publisher.

This publication is designed to provide accurate and authoritative information with regard to the subject matter covered. It is sold with the understanding that the publisher is not engaged in rendering legal, accounting, or other professional advice. If legal advice or other expert assistance is required, the services of a competent professional person should be sought.

—From a *Declaration of Principles* jointly adopted by a Committee of the American Bar Association and a Committee of Publishers and Associations

Many of the designations used by manufacturers and sellers to distinguish their product are claimed as trademarks. Where those designations appear in this book and Adams Media was aware of a trademark claim, the designations have been printed with initial capital letters.

Material from Appendix B has been adapted and abridged from *1001 Ways to Make Money If You Dare* by Trent Hamm, copyright © 2009 by F+W Media Inc., ISBN 10: 1-59869-885-0, ISBN 13: 978-1-59869-885-5.

This book is available at quantity discounts for bulk purchases.
For information, please call 1-800-289-0963.

Dedication

This book is dedicated to all the budding assholes out there who have yet to realize how important they are to society. You make the world go round, asshole. Now read this book and get out there and asshole it up.

Acknowledgments

A book of such dignity and scope doesn't happen by accident, it happens by many accidents, and because of the help and devotion of many people.

Thanks to Grace Freedson, our agent, for getting us this plumb assignment.

Thanks to our wives, Dianne and Jeanne, for putting up with all of our asshole tendencies. (We're not stupid.)

And thanks to all of our asshole teachers, mentors, and role models: You know who you assholes are.

—Steven and Dennis

Disclaimer

You were the one who picked up the book. So you should have an idea as to what you're in for. Being an asshole has its benefits, but it also has its drawbacks. You will be called out. You will be confronted. So you will need to man up. We're here to help you become an asshole, not to hear you complain about how hard it is. If you don't think you're up for the challenge, don't bother.

Becoming an asshole is a lifestyle choice. Your friends and family have to deal with the change. And you have to deal with the consequences—the good and the bad. Don't say we didn't warn you.

Contents

Preface

Assholeology is more than a science. It's an art form. Lucky for you, inside these pages you'll find a crash course in how to excel at adapting to this lifestyle. It will transform you in a way you couldn't even begin to imagine. So rather than limit ourselves to your limited imagination, let's take a look at Kevin. . . .

Kevin is the CEO and owner of a mid-sized company. Kevin went to a good college, an amazing grad school, got his MBA, and after his schooling, he went to work for the company founded by his mother and father. He started in middle management, but, in a very short time, took hold of the daily operations of the entire organization.

He has a good life, a beautiful wife, a gorgeous new house, and two adorable kids. Kevin has a few close friends but a BlackBerry full of contacts and connections. His coworkers and employees think he is a decent boss, but can be kind of a prick in certain situations. He is doing incredibly well for a man of his young age.

There is just something about Kevin that makes him a success. He gives off an aura of confidence that borders on arrogance. He appears more attractive by the way he carries himself in public. He makes an immediate impression on strangers. Some people like him. Some people hate him. Everyone remembers him.

Kevin is an asshole. He does what he wants, when he wants, and makes no apologies or excuses. He doesn't care. It's why his wife married him, why his family let him take over the business, why his employees tolerate his actions, why his friends keep hanging around, and why he is so well connected. Everyone lets it all slide.

Kevin wasn't always this way, though. During college, he was the quiet one in his group of friends. He just went with the flow. Didn't have much luck with women. Wasn't ever really noticed. Until he started working at his parent's company and watching his dad in action. That man could control a room—even beyond the boardroom. When Kevin went out to a restaurant or bar with his dad, everyone wanted to listen to his stories. Everyone wanted to be around him. He was honest, confident, said what was on his mind, and took all the love and hate in stride. In short, he was an asshole. So Kevin worked at mastering the art of assholeology. And lucky for him he succeeded.

Why? Pretty simple. Assholes rule the world.

Read on to learn how you can rule, too.

Part I
Defining the Asshole

Chapter 1
What Makes an Asshole?

Man, she's gorgeous. She came with a small group of friends, but as far as attached goes, she appears single and available. You rarely approach women in bars, but maybe this time . . . oh, man . . . who the hell is that? It's that guy from the line out front. Well, technically, he walked past the line and right inside the bar without even getting off his cell phone. He also got the bartender's attention in a second while you leaned against the bar for ten minutes with your finger in the air, basically begging for service. Why is she talking to him? Does he know her? Are they leaving together? Son of a bitch! What an asshole.

Assholes come in all shapes and sizes. They originate from every background, region, race, and religion. They surround you. There are assholes in your family, in your fantasy football league, and living in the apartment above you (and not just because you keep yelling, "Stop jumping around, asshole!" every night before bed).

You encounter numerous assholes on the average day. Think of the ass-kisser at work that gets bumped up in rank every year even though he is less productive around the office than the armless night janitor. He does little to earn the cushy corner digs and company rank on his business card, yet he is somehow in on every important meeting, every power lunch, and is the first to get invited to every office happy hour. Ponder the Facebook friend that posts pictures of his amazing weekend excursions to places in the world that you couldn't point out on a map or even spell correctly to Google search. He takes vacations and trips he doesn't deserve by mooching off friends, coworkers, and anyone with an empty couch. He never once returns the favor, yet people never seem to mind. Take notice of the guy at the gym who finds a way to flirt, pump, and dump every woman in the evening spin class and still come off looking like a real swell fella. Three prime examples of genuine, 100-percent asshole.

Guess what? Good for them. Assholes have the system beat. They've mastered the art of doing little work, having fun, and getting laid even though the general consensus is that they are total jerks. They have learned to work with the skills they were given and manipulate them to their greatest potential.

Assholes have the system beat.

Ponder this: If assholes are so despised, then why do women still want to be with them and men still want to be like them? Why are books, movies, and television shows about assholes so popular? Why do assholes get noticed in every public situation while guys like you could run through a crowded bar with your pants on fire and not get a drink in the crotch from a good-looking woman or a tackle and pat down from another guy? Simple: You don't stand out. Besides your pants being on fire, you are no different than any other face in the crowd. You are the nice guy no one remembers five minutes after meeting. Assholes are never forgotten.

Why Be an Asshole?

After reading that scenario, the first question that probably popped into your head was, "How did my pants catch fire?" The second (and more relevant) question you probably asked yourself was, "But why would I want to be an asshole?" To better explain the why, let's clear up a misconception about assholes. Assholes are not douche bags; there are assholes and then there are douche bags, and there is a world of difference between the two:

Assholes are never forgotten.

Assholes

The guy at the bar, the jerk at work, the social-networking schmuck, the spin class spinner—those are all prime examples of real assholes. Everything an asshole does is focused on a positive result. They let the ends justify the means. They think their actions through and usually aren't careless or clueless. Sure, some people get burned by the asshole's actions, but as the saying goes, you have to break a few eggs to make an omelet. However, for all the crap assholes pull, they still manage to come off as genuinely likable people. In truth, an asshole is actually a decent person with the innate ability to turn on their asshole charm in the correct situation. For example, the guy at the bar knows that coming off as cocky, confident, and a bit of a jerk will get him into the bar with a drink in his hand and saddled up to a gorgeous woman faster than being a nice guy. But he wouldn't act the same way in the post office or supermarket. Unless he is fighting for the last case of Red Bull—then all bets are off.

Douche Bags

Douche bags are much different than assholes. Douche bags are destructive; they don't think twice about their actions or the ramifications of said actions. A douche bag only thinks of one person: himself. Douche bags will lie, cheat, steal, and cut corners to get exactly what they want out of every situation. No one likes a douche bag, not even his mom.

No one likes a douche bag, not even his mom.

To help make the distinction between assholes and douche bags, let's examine some timeless assholes and give an example of a corresponding douche bag. The following assholes are perfect examples of the successful, powerful, and pioneering asshole. These assholes are trailblazers and specimens to be studied, revered, and emulated. The other guys are just plain douche bags.

ASSHOLE

Denis Leary—Seems like a no-brainer, especially since he's written a song called "Asshole." Leary used his angry and bitter asshole persona to make a name in stand-up comedy and later in television. Because of his likeability—built up by doing things like raising more than $2 million to help fund fire departments through his Leary Firefighters Foundation—he can get away with being an asshole. One well-publicized asshole move came from a claim in his book *Why We Suck* that the rise in autism diagnoses was due to inattentive parents wanting an explanation for why their dumb-ass kids can't compete academically. Still, you gotta love the guy. He's an asshole you'd want to grab a pint and watch the ballgame with.

THE QUOTABLE ASSHOLE
"Why hate someone for the color of their skin when there are much better reasons to hate them."—Denis Leary

DOUCHE BAG

Don Imus—You can be an asshole and say mean things about people as long as you're well liked and funny. The "I-man" is obviously neither. His racist comments about the Rutgers women's basketball team were offensive to the women involved, but also to anyone who calls comedy their profession. If you are going to get fired from your job and publicly raked over the coals at least make the joke funny. It wasn't even accurate or original. It was just a stab at humor by a bitter old douche bag who was always just a poor imitation of more successful radio shock jocks. His cowboy hats—now those are fucking funny.

ASSHOLE

Barney Stinson—Fictional, yes, but he could be the perfect example of a genuine and likable asshole. He is a cocky, conceited, borderline alcoholic, womanizing liar, so all in all a pretty fun dude to be around. Stinson lives life by an unwritten set of rules called "The Bro Code," which provide justification for his actions. As scummy as he seems, people still like him. He has a strong inner circle of pals, even though he slept with one of his female friends who was the ex-girlfriend of his best friend. Barney is the quintessential asshole.

DOUCHE BAG

Spencer Pratt—Pratt is ushering in a new breed of douche bag that become famous just for being douche bags. With little talent and less brains, he and his wife, Heidi Montag, have become two of the most recognized faces in pop culture. He did it by playing up his ultimate douche-bag image whenever the reality cameras were rolling. Is he really that big of a prick or is it all just a clever marketing scheme? Hard to tell. Either way, he is a douche bag for pulling it off so convincingly.

THE QUOTABLE ASSHOLE

"Success is a lousy teacher. It seduces smart people into thinking they can't lose."—Bill Gates

ASSHOLE

Bill Gates—Gates captured the public's attention as a *Revenge of the Nerds*-type asshole CEO in the late '80s. Gates's reputation for annihilating underlings' ideas and egos in staff meetings is legendary. He was able to focus his asshole tendencies and inspire his employees to ride the success of DOS—an operating system invented by someone else—into the creation of the most successful software company in history. You can't get a personal computer to work without Windows. (This is under the assumption you can actually get Windows to work.) Gates ushered in the Internet revolution and changed the way people live and work. He may have been an industry thief and a prick boss, but who wouldn't want to rub elbows with Gates or at least crash at his house for a weekend?

DOUCHE BAG

Donald Trump—"The Donald" is not the richest, the smartest, or the most successful businessman of all time, but the man knew enough about marketing to make his name a brand: Trump Tower, Trump Casino, Trump International Golf Course. And he shamelessly plugs his many ventures any chance he gets on his television show *The Apprentice*. Hell, he even got people to automatically add a "the" in front of his first name for effect. It's crystal clear that this guy's a fluffy-haired douche bag, though not as clear as Trump-brand water. He is the only douche that needs to be fired.

BOUGHT WITH THE DONALD'S DOLLARS

- ☑ Casino
- ☑ Golf course
- ☑ Blazin' third wife
- ☐ Class

THE QUOTABLE ASSHOLE

"Everything negative—pressure, challenges—is all an opportunity for me to rise."—Kobe Bryant

ASSHOLE

Kobe Bryant—Always the overachieving asshole, Bryant skipped over the amateur circuit known as college basketball and headed straight for the NBA after high school. He's nicknamed after a dangerous and feared snake, the black mamba, which strikes quickly and is the fastest land snake in the world. Detractors feel the nickname is also fitting because Bryant is a snake in the grass that paid his way out of a rape accusation and claimed former teammate Shaquille O'Neal once did the same thing. But Bryant always seems to slither out on top. He is a four-time NBA champion, future Hall of Famer, and one of the best to ever play the game. He is an asshole that anyone would love to have on their team. Just get a separate hotel room on road trips.

ass • hole • ol • o • gy

DOUCHE BAG

Barry Bonds—Imagine being considered one of the best athletes in your respective sport. A certified star who would go down in the record books as perhaps one of the greatest to ever set foot on the field. Now think about being such a giant douche bag that all of that isn't good enough, so you (allegedly) take human growth hormone, experience a career rejuvenation past your prime, and smash the records of some of the most beloved names in your sport, your legend getting almost as large as your newly enlarged noggin. Barry Bonds changed the way the public will forever view successful, and drug-free, baseball players. Guilty until proven innocent. All thanks to one big egotistical douche bag. Even Barry Bonds would hate playing with Barry Bonds.

As you can see, assholes are successful, well connected, take what they want in life, and have the system by the pocket nuggets. But now you're probably saying that all these guys are famous and that's why they can get away with being assholes. Why would *you* want to be an asshole?

Take a minute for a quick exercise: Close your eyes. Name the first asshole that comes to mind. It didn't take long did it? In fact, you thought of at least three in just that short time. Are they well liked? Do they get what they want? Now ask yourself, if it were possible, if you would like to be able to do that. Would you switch places if you could? You are allowed to say yes. It's the correct answer. Get *something* right for once.

Assholes are successful, well connected, take what they want in life, and have the system by the pocket nuggets.

There is nothing wrong with wanting to be an asshole. Assholes are always surrounded by a solid group of people; the ying to their giant, egotistical yang. They have a certain likeability that makes people want to be around them. They are never left out of the crowd. Every party, event, and function—the asshole isn't just in attendance, he's the first to get invited. It's usually you who is left standing on the outside and wanting so desperately to be let in.

Have What It Takes?

Not everyone can be an asshole. This is good; the last thing the world needs is to be chock full of assholes. Somebody has to be the nice guy. Someone needs to fill the role of guy that gets stepped on by the assholes climbing to the top. Someone has to run around the bar with their cotton Dockers on fire because, frankly, there is nothing an asshole likes better than a good laugh at the expense of others. There is nothing to be ashamed of if you think you can't handle being an asshole. Enjoy your mediocre life of going to bed by 10:00 P.M. on the weekdays and talking yourself into starting that model-car blog. Send us the URL when it's up and running. Do you have our e-mail? No? Cool.

> You will have to take every negative thing said about you and let it bounce off your chest.

For the aspiring assholes, this is the time for some soul searching. You are going to change the way you approach even the simplest situation. You will have to forget everything your mother ever taught you about common courtesy and humbleness. You will have to look yourself in the mirror every morning and say, "I'm ready to show the world what an asshole I can be."

Here are three essential things every asshole must have:

1. **Thick skin:** Get ready to be disliked by a large majority of the people you come in contact with on a daily basis. You will have to take every negative thing said about you and let it bounce off your chest like Superman does hollow tips. There will be detractors, haters, and people who will want to drag your name (and your face) through the mud every chance they get. You have to roll with the negative and remain positive. They only dislike you because they want to be you. It's not going to kill you; it'll only make you stronger. Unless someone physically comes after you for being such a prick. Then it may kill you.

2. **The ability to say no to anyone:** It's the greatest word in an asshole's vocabulary. Master the art of saying no and you will unlock doors and opportunities that you never dreamed possible. It's not no to everything, just no to all the things you hate doing: family obligations, girlfriend/wife situations, tasks at work, or anything that just plain sucks. Get it out of your life. It's hard to say no, especially to family and friends, so it will take some practice. Start small with telemarketers and retail people: "No, I don't want a cologne sample. I sweat out awesome." Just say no.

THE QUOTABLE ASSHOLE
"I wipe my ass with your feelings."—Tony Soprano,
The Sopranos

3. **Confidence coming out of, well, your ass:** It's hard to master confidence. Some are born with more than enough and others need to build it over time. It will take some training to be the most confident asshole possible. Even the most successful asshole

has their confidence shaken at some point in life. No matter what happens though the asshole doesn't let it put a chink in his armor. If it does, he'll just go out and buy new armor; the expensive shit that is super shiny and makes him look like an even bigger asshole. See how good he is at maintaining his asshole status?

FIVE THINGS YOU SHOULD *NEVER* BRAG ABOUT
1. Your bank account
2. Your clever quips on Twitter
3. Your fantasy anything team
4. How much you can bench
5. Your bowel movements

Get Ready

Purchasing this book and reading this far means there is a part of you that wants to experience a change. If you've made it to this point, chances are nothing in the coming chapters will scare you away. You will soon be on your way to attaining an extreme level of assholeness.

THE QUOTABLE ASSHOLE
"Call me Helen Keller because I'm a fucking miracle worker!"—Ari Gold, *Entourage*

Are you ready to take the next step? Are you ready to change your life? This is the start of something huge. You are embarking on a wonderful and magical journey, full of self-exploration, personal reflection, and . . . fuck it . . . we have a lot of work to do, let's just get cracking before we all change our minds.

Let's go transform you into a real asshole!

Wait.

Change your pants first.

CHAPTER RECAP: What Makes an Asshole?

Being called an asshole isn't a bad thing. Remember that. It's going to be important throughout the rest of this book and for the rest of your life as an asshole. In life, there are assholes and there are douche bags. Both types of people are in your office, belong to your gym, and can be seen on your television. It's up to you to choose which one you are going to be. If you make the right choice—being an asshole—you will need three things: a thick skin, the ability to say "no" to anyone, and confidence . . . *lots* of confidence.

Ass • hole • ol • o • gy Vocabulary

Asshole (n.): A person who gets what he wants when he wants without acting like a douche bag

Douche bag (n.): A person who no one likes

Likability (n.): A quality a person has that allows his actions to be excused because people enjoy being around him

Character Study

Denis Leary: Born in Worcester, Massachusetts, Leary is an asshole's asshole. Comedian, actor, writer, and philanthropist, he not only gives it to whoever deserves it with his acerbic wit, he also gives back through his charitable foundation. He can get away with being an asshole because of his likability.

Questions to Think About

- Who do you think of when you hear the word "asshole"? And what can you learn from them?
- What's the difference between an asshole and a douche bag?
- Why do you want to be an asshole?

What You *Should* Have Learned

- ❑ Assholes have the system beat.
- ❑ Douche bags are hated—even by their moms.
- ❑ It's okay to be cocky as long as you're not too cocky.
- ❑ Spencer Pratt is a douche bag.
- ❑ You have to be able to take it if you plan on giving it.

Chapter 2
The Evolution of the Asshole

Being an asshole is not new. The asshole shows up frequently throughout history—from the early days of the Bible right up to the war with Iraq. History is littered with assholes that imposed their will on thousands, sometimes millions, of people just to satisfy their own needs. Let's discuss some of the most influential assholes throughout history and how they affected the modern-day asshole.

THE 'HOLE TRUTH

George Santayana once said, "Those who cannot learn from history are doomed to repeat it." He probably meant in summer school.

Assholes Through the Ages: A Timeline

The following men are perfect examples of the successful, powerful, pioneering, and timeless asshole. Their accomplishments and legacies will last long into the next several centuries. These assholes are trailblazers in their fields and specimens to be studied, revered, and emulated.

Pharaoh Khufu (2589 B.C.–2566 B.C.)

The man behind the pyramid: Khufu is the Egyptian ruler who commissioned the Great Pyramid of Giza. It's been revealed that the douche-bag move of wrangling slaves to construct this stone monstrosity is probably untrue; instead, Khufu used his pull as an asshole to have tens of thousands of Egyptians sign up to sling rocks. You can't even get a friend to help you dig out a patio, even with the bribe of a thirty-pack. Looks like Pharaoh Khufu could teach you a thing or two.

So maybe it was a little extreme to work even the willing to death, but this Pharaoh got the job done. And what does he have to show for it? Oh, nothing much; just one of the Seven Wonders of the ancient world. Is there any other reason to visit Egypt besides seeing the pyramids? I can't believe you just said, "For the shopping."

Those who hated him never told him to his face—the sign of a true asshole.

Mark Antony (83 B.C.–30 B.C.)

Some loved him, some hated him, but those who hated him never told him to his face—the sign of a true asshole. Caesar's second in command managed to win accolades as a famous military leader, yet a reputation for his infamous spells of debauchery are just as legendary.

While he might have been just a little late warning Caesar about the whole assassination thing, his speech at the ruler's funeral turned the tides on the backstabbers and got his fellow Romans after those douche bags. Even though he might not always have been a stand-up guy, he was definitely upfront about it. And that whole "helped to cause the fall of the Roman Empire" thing can be countered with the fact that he bedded Cleopatra.

Charlemagne (742–814)

This pillaging asshole may have let his lust for land get a little out of hand, but his rampaging conquest is credited with a huge revival in art, religion, and culture. Through his foreign invasions, internal actions, and general ass kicking, Charlemagne helped define both Western Europe and the Middle Ages. Today he is regarded as the father of Europe. Under his thumb, the empire united most of Western Europe, which gives us the wonderful European treasures we love today—the Eiffel Tower, Big Ben, and the Amsterdam Red Light District.

Genghis Khan (1162–1227)

You can't build the largest empire in history and not be an asshole. Genghis not only kicked ass ruthlessly, he also brought many nomadic tribes under one banner. His power of persuasion definitely shows off the fact that people wanted to be around him (granted, they were also probably scared shitless of him).

Henry VIII (1491–1547)

In true asshole fashion, when Henry wanted something he would stop at nothing to get it. Create his own church? Sure. Kill off his wives? Why not? All this guy wanted to do was produce a male heir to continue his legacy. Sure, his methods were a little extreme and he went through wives like most men do bottles of Jergens, but you can't fault a guy for trying. This historical asshole may have let personal get in front of professional, but he shows that no one should let anything or anyone get in the way of their goals (not even the Pope).

John Hancock (1737–1793)

A lot of words were tossed around back in the d-a-y to describe John Hancock: criminal, smuggler, pirate. All were used as jabs against this one-time merchant turned politician, but none of that matters now since he was on our side. We just recognize him as an important player in the Revolution who took joy in pissing off King George. It's even been said that the reason he made his signature so large on the Declaration of Independence was so Georgey could read it without his glasses. Now *that's* an asshole move we can believe in.

A true American asshole.

Wild Bill Hickok (1837–1876)

The most badass asshole on this timeline (sorry Genghis), Wild Bill ruled the Old West with his own code of conduct. Similar to Mark Antony's feats as both a military man and a debaucherous glutton, Wild Bill was both a lawman and a gambler, equally noted and notorious for both. Bill was a master of the quick draw, but he didn't let his skills go to his head—he just made them known. In response to a saloon owner (whom he later killed in a shootout) who claimed he could "kill a crow on the wing," Bill laid it out for the man, saying, "Did the crow have a pistol? Was he shooting back? I will be."

Thomas Edison (1847–1931)

Edison was known as a crotchety old bastard, hard on his employees, and dismissive (at best) of his competitors. He wasn't adverse to stealing ideas, cheating his business partners, or electrocuting elephants. Despite his many faults, later re-creations of several of his patents are still in use today: the phonograph, the light bulb, electricity, and the best thing to happen to sex since contraception—the motion picture camera. Edison is partly responsible for porn. Let that soak in for a minute.

General George Patton (1885–1945)

Commander of the United States 3rd Army during World War II, Patton was famous for being one of the most self-aggrandizing, arrogant, insubordinate assholes in the world. He famously slapped a soldier suffering from shellshock while visiting an army hospital unit and almost lost his career because of it. However, when Eisenhower wanted someone to break through the German front and rip the heart out of the Nazi war machine, he called our own jodhpur-wearing, pearl-handled-revolver toting, asshole general. Stand at attention soldiers, there is a four-star asshole in the room.

THE QUOTABLE ASSHOLE

"Attitude is a little thing that makes a big difference."
—Winston Churchill

Winston Churchill (1874–1965)

British officer, politician, writer, asshole—Churchill was the real deal. The leader of Great Britain during World War II, he showcased his grace under pressure, an important part of the asshole's A-game. He was also known for some great comebacks, and not the kind he pulled off in '51 after reclaiming his position as Prime Minister after being defeated in '45. No, Churchill was a master of repartee, like in this exchange with Lady Astor, the first female Member of Parliament:

Lady Astor: "Winston, you're drunk!"
Churchill: "Yes, I am, and you, madam, are ugly. But I'll be sober in the morning."

Take a page from Churchill's playbook and use that one the next time the missus complains about your drinking . . . if you're ballsy enough.

So what do these historical assholes teach us? The first thing that is obvious is that being an asshole is forgiven over time if the outcome is beneficial to more than a handful of people. Think of how history celebrates the inventions of Edison or how Hollywood portrayed the character of Patton. Sure, the negative is mentioned, but the success is celebrated.

Second, if it weren't for assholes, the world wouldn't have made such impressive advances in art, religion, literature, architecture, or even warfare and the managing of men for a greater goal. You can shake your head at the way they approached each project but you can't disagree that the end result is impressive, if not monumental, in scope and scale.

> If it weren't for assholes, the world wouldn't have made such impressive advances.

Find the Asshole in Your Genes

Gregor Mendel was a priest, scientist, and "The Father of Genetics." (Talk about a triple threat.) His genetic experiments with peapods showed how round peas held a recessive gene that, in the right combinations, could lead to a dented pea. When Mendel presented his paper, "Experiments on Plant Hybridization," to the Natural History Society of Brünn in Moravia in 1865, he set the scientific world, ironically, on its ass. His findings revealed that combinations of genes passed down through generations consistently affected traits in the offspring. The dents were passed down.

Two important questions stem from Mendel's work:

1. Is the asshole gene hereditary?
2. Didn't eighteenth-century scientists have anything better to do than experiment on peas?

NOTE: *This isn't going to turn into a biology lesson. (We all slept through that the first time around.) What we will discuss is the role genealogy plays in you being an asshole.*

To speak to question number one—we'll let you ponder number two on your own time—a gene is defined as the unit of inheritance passed from parent to offspring. It's a sequence of DNA contained by and arranged linearly along a chromosome. Each gene transmits different chemical information known as a trait. Could being an asshole be in your genes? Can the traits of an asshole be passed down?

Frankly, no. You could come from a line of assholes and not be smart enough to learn the family business or have been spawned from a long line of pushovers and have what it takes to excel at being a top-notch prick. Any individual can attain the asshole attitude as long as they are open to the experience and are willing to do what is needed to succeed. While a family full of assholes doesn't hurt your chances at picking up the persona, you aren't necessarily stuck in the land of mediocrity if the men in your family are less intimidating than the women.

Any individual can attain the asshole attitude.

ASSHOLE IN ACTION: Stan

Stan was the leader of the group. He had been since child-hood. This was based on two reasons: he was the tallest and had the biggest set of balls in the group. The first part was all genetics and because he hung with a bunch of undersized thugs. Being much more assertive than the rest of the brood developed over time. In fact, even after all these years, well into retirement age, Stan was still a huge prick if the situation demanded.

Take last week, for example. The bar was mobbed for a Thursday afternoon—the normal golf crew plus some local convention crashing from the hotel across the street. Stan just spent the afternoon chasing his ball all over God's green earth (also known as Springdale Country Golf Course) and was in a foul mood. The bartender yapping to a bunch of out-of-towners at the opposite end of the bar wasn't getting a drink in Stan's hand anytime soon. He waited for one more moment and then took action.

Not everyone can embrace the asshole mentality.

Stan reached into his pocket for his cell and called infor-mation. He asked for the number of Tony's Tavern on Bruns-wick Ave. The phone at the bar rang. Stan watched as the bartender pulled himself away from the chatter to answer the phone.

"Tony's!" the barkeep yelled into the mouthpiece.

"Yeah," said Stan "this is the people at the other end of the bar. When you're done chatting we could all use a drink."

The Nature-Versus-Nurture Argument

For years, the question of whether the asshole gene is learned or inbred has kept researchers up at night. It's the nature-versus-nurture conundrum at its best. Is it heredity or the environment that most impacts human psychological development? While we just established that an asshole lineage does not secure a spot at the a-hole table, there is something to be said about those lucky enough to be nurtured in the school of thought.

⊢ THE 'HOLE TRUTH ⊢

When we said "years" and "researchers," we actually meant "one night over a couple beers" and "us alcoholic authors." It's the findings that matter, though!

No child is an asshole at birth. A baby isn't born giving orders, being assertive, and setting goals for a successful life. Being an asshole is a learned discipline. It's taught either by a successful asshole or through a child's own adventures in trial and error. When a child is hungry, does the smile-and-laugh approach get them food? No. Does the cry-until-some-eardrums-bleed approach get results? Of course. The child learns what works and what doesn't and from there he decides how and when to use those powers.

Nature created the need for an asshole. Nurturing brought the asshole to life.

Will Assholes Become the Norm?

Natural selection is the process by which heritable traits that make it more likely for an organism to survive and reproduce become more common in a population over generations. In other words, the smart ones adapt while the dumbasses die off.

Does that mean assholes are eventually going to become the dominant species? Will people come to realize that the asshole behavior is crucial for survival and advancement? Will the world be overrun with assholes? No. Just like there must be species that don't catch on as quickly, there must be nice people and douche bags roaming the earth. Not everyone can embrace the asshole mentality; it will have its detractors, naysayers, and people that just aren't any good at it. Sucks for them.

Being an asshole is a learned discipline.

CHAPTER RECAP: The Evolution of the Asshole

Assholes have been around for a long time. And like with any group of people, you can learn a lot by studying their history. Whether it's Mark Antony's womanizing ways or Winston Churchill's quick wit, there's plenty to gain from looking to the assholes of the past. You can even learn a thing or two from your own family tree. However, just because there are assholes in your family lineage doesn't mean the persona is going to be passed on genetically. You need to learn how to be an asshole.

Ass • hole • ol • o • gy Vocabulary

Debaucherous (adj.): Indulging in every way possible; also see: "having fun"

Repartee (n.): A clever retort used when someone hates on you

Natural selection (n.): The process in which the weak are picked off and the strong survive

Character Study

Wild Bill Hickok: A frontiersman of the Wild West, Hickok was the real deal. Even though he was a supreme badass, he also helped to uphold the law in a lawless society. That took some serious balls. To further your character study, rent or buy *Deadwood* on DVD and watch the dramatic interpretation of his asshole life. (Not like you have anything better to do.)

Questions to Think About
- Who is your favorite asshole in history? Why?
- Who is your least favorite douche bag in history? Why?
- What asshole traits did you learn growing up?

What You *Should* Have Learned
❑ History is full of assholes. Very successful and world-changing assholes.
❑ Your entire time in school you learned about a ton of assholes, you just didn't realize it until now. Don't you wish you had paid closer attention?
❑ Scientists have a hard-on for peas.
❑ It really doesn't matter if you have a family full of assholes or none on the tree—being an asshole isn't hereditary.
❑ No one is born an asshole; it's a learned trait.
❑ The world won't be overrun with assholes—someone needs to be at the bottom of the pecking order. Don't let it be you.
❑ There are assholes doing things now that our children and grandchildren will be learning about years from now. Warms the heart.

Chapter 3
The Asshole's Ten Demandments

Now that we've explained the what and the why of being an asshole, it's time to get into the how. How does one act like an asshole? How does a person keep from becoming a douche bag? How does one know the difference?

In the next few chapters, we will explain the asshole's approach to everything from business and pleasure to relationships and family. Before we get to all that though, it's important to explain the rules of being an asshole.

THE QUOTABLE ASSHOLE

"I've always been considered an asshole for about as long as I can remember. That's just my style."—Royal Tenenbaum, *The Royal Tenenbaums*

Long ago, way back when, not quite biblical times but *way* before indoor toilets, the automobile, and those delicious Girl Scout Thin Mints, several men sat down and drafted the principles and rules of what it means to be an asshole. The governing body of Assholeology, the Demandments lay out the groundwork for the persona you must assume in order to get away with being an asshole. Fast forward the DVR to modern times: You can replace the "thy," "thee," and "shall," but the fundamentals remain the same, allowing you to achieve being an asshole in today's world with its indoor plumbing, hybrid SUVs, and those delicious fucking Thin Mints. (Have you ever put them in the freezer? Do it. Like an orgasm in a silver sleeve.)

The asshole lives by ten simple rules: The Asshole's Ten Demandments.

And so here they are, the ten simple rules the asshole lives by: The Asshole's Ten Demandments. These rules don't command a person to do anything. That choice is ultimately up to the individual. They do however demand that if a person chooses to follow the Ten Demandments, they adhere to every single demandment to reach an ultimate goal.

THE ASSHOLE'S TEN DEMANDMENTS

I. The asshole cares about the asshole the most.
Life isn't always fair. It's occasionally cruel. And an asshole learns that eventually other people will disappoint. They don't mean to, but it's part of human nature. It's because of this fact that the asshole must think of himself first. The asshole is always the most important person in any situation. With every decision and opportunity the asshole asks internally, "How does this benefit me?" "What

do I stand to gain?" and "How can I make the most of this situation?" The phrase "What's in it for me?" was likely coined by an asshole.

II. The asshole is always right.

Most people think they are right. The asshole knows he is right. Every time. He will go to extremes to prove his point. Even when the debate seems to be coming to an end, and in the favor of the other person, the asshole will not let it go until he is proven correct. Even when all facts prove the asshole wrong, in the asshole's mind, he is still 100-percent correct. An eventual surrender from the other side will also suffice.

ASSHOLE IN ACTION: professor brown

Professor Brown demanded results from each of his students. He was known around campus as a prick, but always had full classes.

One afternoon during class, his students were going around the room explaining the extracurricular activities they were involved in on campus like the college radio station, the newspaper, and various other clubs and groups.

The discussion comes around to a girl on the basketball team. She wasn't the star of the team but was better than the average female player. The professor asked her what she did besides basketball. She explained that basketball took up all of her time so she didn't get involved in any extracurricular activities. She said she wanted to play in the WNBA. Professor Brown just said, "Oh, ok" and moved on to the next student.

At the next class, waiting on her desk was a printout of the number of players who play women's college basketball each season and the number of women that make a WNBA roster.

Underneath that information were sign-up sheets for different student groups on campus.

She joined the college radio station that afternoon.

III. The asshole rarely apologizes.

"Sorry" isn't a part of the asshole's vocabulary. Sure he has used it on a few occasions—like when he accidentally bumped into someone on the subway or when he was found out for sleeping with all the women in his friend's family—but even in those moments he really doesn't mean he is regretful. He means, "Sorry you weren't lucky enough to rub against me longer" or "Sorry your family genes couldn't produce more women for me to bed." There is never anything to be sorry about if the asshole is never wrong.

THE QUOTABLE ASSHOLE

"Be a yardstick of quality. Some people aren't used to an environment where excellence is expected."—Steve Jobs

---

IV. The asshole never accepts the word "no."

While an asshole never uses the word "sorry," neither does he accept the word "no." No doesn't exist in the world of the asshole. It's just yes: Yes to his wishes. Yes to his demands. Yes to his place for drinks after dinner. If he does hear the word no, he turns it into yes. (The only exception: When a particular no really does mean no. That situation shouldn't have to be explained.)

V. The asshole is always in control.

The asshole is in complete command in every situation—in the boardroom, the bar room, and the bedroom. He steps up to take charge and doesn't look for help unless absolutely necessary. The asshole stays cool, calm, and collected.

VI. The asshole always has a plan.

The asshole didn't get to the top based solely on luck and clichés. The asshole always has short-term and long-term goals, and he plots the exact steps required to reach those goals. He is methodical in his approach. If things don't go according to plan (usually the fault of others), the asshole always has a Plan B.

VII. The asshole takes what he wants.

The asshole never asks, he takes. The people who ask never get exactly what they want. The asshole always gets what he wants—the nicer office, the bigger slice of cake, the best out of life.

VIII. The asshole always looks good.

There are no occasions when an asshole isn't on his game, in public or in private. The asshole always looks his best. Clothes are the extension of the man. Therefore, the asshole is always spot on. He doesn't have to be a trendsetter, but the asshole is never out of style.

IX. The asshole learns from his (few) mistakes.

An asshole would never be pompous enough to claim perfection—no man is perfect. He does learn from the mistakes he makes in life, though. And he *never* makes the same mistake twice. The asshole's motto: Trick me once, shame on you. Trick me twice? Won't happen. You're lucky you tricked me once.

X. The asshole is always evolving.

The asshole never stops learning, growing, expanding, or experiencing everything life has to offer. When a person stops evolving, they start dying. An asshole will live forever. (Well, at least longer than you.)

Learn these Demandments. Memorize them. Print them on a piece of paper and carry them around in your pocket. If a situation arises where you just don't know what to do or what the next course of action is, refer to the Demandments. They hold all the answers.

THE 'HOLE TRUTH

Get the sheet of paper laminated. Your hands are going to be sweaty the first few times. The last thing you need is to look like a douche bag with ink all over his hands.

Crawl Before You Walk

These Demandments will take time to master. Some are much harder than others to learn and execute. You must crawl before you walk. Here are some suggestions on how to ease into the transition of being an asshole.

Start Small

When you first learned to ride a bike without training wheels, your parents probably took you over to a soft, grassy area, walked alongside as you pedaled, and let go when they felt the time was right. They didn't just take you out to a busy street and yell, "Start pedaling!" They eased you into riding without training wheels. Sure you fell the first few times, but after a while you were pedaling by yourself. Then you realized you were going to be late for work and told your mom to have dinner ready before *Battlestar Galactica*.

Take baby steps when first beginning the asshole process. Pick situations where you would feel the most comfortable displaying your new attitude. Don't walk into every situation with a new, abrasive attitude; it will backfire faster than your first car. Let's say, for example, you go to breakfast every morning at the same small shop, but at least nine breakfast sandwiches out of ten they get the order wrong. Normally, you just eat the incorrect order and hope they get it right the next time. Instead of eating more bacon than humanly acceptable, open the sandwich in front of them and explain that you didn't order bacon and that you expect the order to be fixed. Sure, you're getting some pubes in your egg yolks—*so don't eat the sandwich*—but stand up for yourself and your arteries. Pick your spots.

Take baby steps when first beginning the asshole process.

Track Your Progress

If you started a new workout routine, signed up for a writing class, or even started a new job, the first thing you would do is take notes. It's impossible to remember everything. Important things must be written down. Just like every new venture, routine, or class you have to take field notes to learn from and study for future reference. Jot down little suggestions or reminders after each encounter. Take note of minor details and what worked and didn't work in certain situations. Take special notice of people's reactions and responses and what you did or said to take control of the situation. Chart your progress and compare notes three, six, and nine months down the line. The notebook is a valuable learning tool.

⊢ THE 'HOLE TRUTH ⊢

Keep the notebook in a safe place. Pretend it's like the diary you kept in high school. Minus the Hello Kitty cover.

Find a Mentor

This book is a wonderful learning tool, but nothing is more valuable than a good teacher. There must be an asshole in your life that you admire. If you don't have an asshole close to you, seek one out and ask for their assistance. Don't approach with the question of, "How can I be an asshole like you?" because you'll probably get punched in the mouth. Angle it so that it's an interesting proposition: "I was curious as to how you learned to be so assertive and such a commanding presence." Explain your situation and how you hope to learn something from his years of experience. A little ego stroking never hurt anyone.

An asshole only becomes an asshole by applying the Demandments to all situations.

Practice

Practice doesn't just make perfect, it makes permanent. The only way to get practice is to get into situations that require execution of as many of the Demandments as possible. An asshole only becomes an asshole by applying the Demandments to all situations. Eventually, it will go beyond breakfast sandwiches. This means you'll have to enter into some uncomfortable scenarios that you previously would have handled much differently or avoided completely. If the situation doesn't work out to your liking, try it again—and again and again—until you have an answer for everything. As your confidence builds you will begin to approach every situation with an asshole mentality.

You're Going to Be an Asshole: Time to Warn Others

It's a crisp, fall day; brisk morning air gives way to a warm, picturesque afternoon. You have a ton of chores, but they are all thrown on the back-burner. Instead, it's a quick bike ride for some exercise, a munchies run, and an afternoon of football on the tube and power napping in your recliner.

Suddenly your cell blows up like Tyra Banks's ass. It's your friend. He leaves a message on your voicemail saying he's moving in with his girlfriend today and could really use an extra hand lifting some ridiculously heavy furniture up three flights of stairs. He promises it won't take that long or be as bad as it seems. He is obviously a terrible liar.

You have two options (surprisingly, neither of them is actually helping the guy out):

Option #1: Don't return the phone call and hope he finds some other sucker to help. This also involves lying when you finally speak again. That is, if you ever hear from him after he is done moving.

Option #2: Call him back, tell him you'd love to help him move that furniture, but it sounds like a pretty shitty way to spend a good afternoon and you'll decline the offer. It's an asshole move, but at least it's honest.

On most occasions, honesty is the best policy. Unfortunately, honesty makes you seem like an incredibly selfish asshole. It comes with the territory. The asshole attitude and approach works in all parts of life.

It's an asshole move, but at least it's honest.

Even though it's sometimes impossible to disconnect from life, occasionally turning off all contact with the outside world is necessary. Basically, hide.

Your friends know you better than you know yourself. They understand what makes you tick. Changing your approach to life and becoming an asshole will be a hard sell to those closest to you. A true friend will understand and accept the fact that in order for your life to take a vastly different course you must change your attitude.

FIVE FAVORS YOU SHOULD *NEVER* AGREE TO

1. **Moving:** An asshole doesn't lift his own couch, let alone someone else's.
2. **Painting:** It's a legal form of torture that should definitely be outlawed.
3. **Pet sitting:** Your friend goes away for the weekend, leaving you to take care of Doodles while it manages its abandonment issues by dropping a hot brownie on your sofa.
4. **Airport pick up/drop off:** This doesn't need an explanation.
5. **Lending money:** It never, *ever* ends well.

Here's how to break the news.

1. **Be honest.** This new approach to life will be a shock to friends and family. It's no different than choosing a new religion or a change in diet. Imagine if you said to your former Catholic school friends, "I think I'm going to give this Buddhism a shot" or admitted to the guys that red meat is killing from the inside out and it's nothing but bean stalks and turnips for you. Your friends would bust your chops incessantly but ultimately

understand your change of heart. Why is being an asshole such an odd lifestyle change? You want to experience the best in life and that only comes from doing things on your own terms. It's a religion, a philosophy, and a way of life all wrapped into one. Minus the turnips.

THE QUOTABLE ASSHOLE

"Pain or damage don't end the world. Or despair or fucking beatings. The world ends when you're dead. Until then, you got more punishment in store. Stand it like a man . . . and give some back."—Al Swearengen, *Deadwood*

2. **Be blunt.** The choice to be an asshole may be met with some trepidation and backtalk: "Why would you want to be an asshole?" they'll ask. This just means they don't get it, so instead of arguing and debating all day just be blunt and end the discussion: "This is my choice. I've given it some thought and it's for the best. Back off." It will sting, but it beats the debate. Really sell it with the "Back off." Think Yosemite Sam on a tire mud flap.

3. **Still be a friend.** A new approach to life doesn't mean you start walking all over the people that matter the most. They will stick around whether you ascend to new heights or fall flat on your . . . wait for it . . . asshole. They are still the most important people in your life. Never forget the little dingle berries. (Sorry, one asshole pun per section, it's in the contract.)

Be assertive. Be patient. Be thorough.

It's important not to lose hope or sight of the ultimate goal. There will be setbacks and situations that may get out of hand. You may lose friends and be shunned by family. Don't let it stop you. Be assertive. Be patient. Be thorough. Be the biggest asshole you can be. It will take time. Remember, Rome wasn't built in a day.

THE 'HOLE TRUTH

Probably because it was impossible to get work done in togas. Hell, it's hard enough just to party in them.

CHAPTER RECAP: The Asshole's Ten Demandments

There are rules. Learn them. Recite them. Live them. Assholeology isn't some lawless philosophy; there is already enough of those in the world. Therefore you need to adopt these rules into your everyday life. But start slowly. You need to crawl before you can walk. Also you need to tell your friends and family about your forthcoming transformation—or else they're likely to walk out on you. Just be honest and shoot them straight. As long as you're living by the code, everything should go fine.

Ass • hole • ol • o • gy Vocabulary

Demandment (n.): A tenet of Assholeology that dictates how an asshole should act

Thin Mint (n.): A minty, mind-blowing cookie

Ego stroking (n.): The act of building another asshole's self-worth by telling him how awesome everything he's accomplished is; the act should be reciprocated

Character Study

Moses: Okay, you caught us. We sort of borrowed the Ten Demandment thing. So it's only fair we shout out the guy who dropped the original Commandment knowledge. While a prophet, Moses was an asshole—in the most non-sacrilegious sense. This guy stood up for what he believed in. Followed his mentor Yahweh to success (with a little ego stroking). And then made his people walk through the desert for a long time.

Questions to Think About
- Which will be the hardest Demandment to follow? Why?
- Who will you choose as your mentor? For what reason(s)?
- How will you break the news of your transformation to your friends?

What You *Should* Have Learned
- ❑ Just like the rules we live by in life, the rules of being an asshole started very early in man's evolution.
- ❑ The Ten Demandments
- ❑ Frozen Thin Mints are awesome.
- ❑ Go slowly. Your transformation isn't going to happen overnight.
- ❑ Keep track of your progress in order to learn from your mistakes.
- ❑ Other people should know of your plans to become an asshole. It's just courtesy.
- ❑ Lessons can be learned from novelty mud flaps.

Part II
Becoming an Asshole

Chapter 4
What Type of
Asshole Are You?

Now that you've got a firm grasp on the Demandments and you've squared this new philosophy away with friends and family, it's time to make another important decision. When you were a kid, people loved to ask you, "What do you want to be when you grow up?" The older you got the more specific the job. It started as a baseball player then it was shortstop for the Cubs. Then the harsh reality hit you like a fastball to the yambag: You didn't even have enough talent to wash the jocks of the varsity baseball team. So you got even more specific and admitted you just wanted a job that got you home in time to watch the baseball game and drown your sorrows in a bucket of scotch.

Success erases the memory of an asshole's detractors.

It's the same concept when deciding to be an asshole. Every field of study has different areas of specialty and expertise. There is a huge difference between a carpenter and ironworker. They aren't just doctors they are pediatricians and proctologists. There are actual gynecologists and those of us that just practice on weekends. It's all about finding your niche.

It's all about finding your niche.

ASK YOURSELF THESE QUESTIONS TO GAIN SOME CLARITY:
What do I want to accomplish?
What are my goals?
What areas of my life need the most work?

THE 'HOLE TRUTH

Save these self-reflecting questions for when you are alone and in front of the mirror. Don't go muttering these to yourself on the subway or in line at Dunkin' Donuts. You will sound like an idiot. More so than usual.

When you decide what you want to accomplish with this attitude change, you can move on to discover the different types of assholes people encounter in their daily lives.

There are certain aspects of life in which an asshole excels.

The Typical Assholes

While being an asshole affects every part of your being, there are certain aspects of life in which an asshole excels. These are the asshole's disciplines. Think of the guy in the office that everyone hates yet crowds around at the Christmas party or the asshole at the party that always finds a way to get everyone to sing along as he plays the piano. (Where the hell do all those pianos keep coming from anyway?)

Here are some common assholes along with the secrets to their success and what you can learn from each.

The Office Asshole

The office asshole is involved in every part of the business: the actual work, the decisions, the lives of coworkers, and the office's extracurricular activities. This asshole knows how connected, and sometimes indispensable, he is in the office, so he's comfortable throwing his weight around. If he isn't included, he finds a way to get himself involved, usually pushing himself to the front of the line. The office asshole also finds a way to get out of as much work as he offers to complete, and knows every loophole to every office rule.

The office asshole knows every loophole to every office rule.

If the asshole is the boss he can do all of the above plus be the end all, be all of every decision and conflict. For the asshole boss, this isn't a job; it's his life.

His Secret

This asshole knows business is business. He will do anything to get ahead and believes the ends will (usually) justify the means.

What You Can Learn

The most important lesson to learn from this asshole is not to take anything personally. Never get emotionally involved in the office or you will never make it to the top of the heap.

THE QUOTABLE ASSHOLE

"Entrepreneurs are simply those who understand that there is little difference between obstacle and opportunity and are able to turn both to their advantage."—Niccolò Machiavelli

The Social Asshole

This asshole is at his best during social functions: at bars, corporate gatherings, sports games, and anything else that involves talking to countless people about hundreds of different topics. He is great at small talk. He is better at networking. Everyone remembers meeting this asshole because he remembers everything about the meeting: "How's the wife? Kids still playing tee-ball? Did Uncle Al ever get that hip replacement?"

His Secret

This asshole is great at listening and remembering. He files even the smallest detail in his mental Rolodex. People love it when you remember little things about them and can make interactions personal.

What You Can Learn

Social skills are incredibly important to the asshole. Talking and listening are his keys to success. A strong memory doesn't hurt either. If you can remember your fantasy-football stats from last season, you can remember the name of a client's wife.

THE 'HOLE TRUTH

No one cares about your fantasy team.

The Athlete Asshole

This asshole has a legitimate excuse for his actions and attitude: He has lived a life of privilege. He has been expected to do nothing but concentrate on his sport while other people tended to everything else in his life. This asshole can be forgiven by 99 percent of the general population because he can bounce a ball or swim faster than a fish. Eventually, he will get paid an incredible amount of money because of that talent. This will make him an even bigger asshole. He will then only feel the love of 95 percent of the general population.

THE QUOTABLE ASSHOLE

"I had to fight all my life to survive. They were all against me . . . but I beat the bastards and left them in the ditch." —Ty Cobb

---

His Secret

HGH. Kidding. It's not really a secret that society makes sports stars celebrities and millionaires just based on athletic talent. It's kind of sad actually, for everyone except the asshole.

What You Can Learn

The asshole attitude is acceptable as long as it makes other people happy. The asshole quarterback can be a jerk to the media, ignore fans, and damage more women than a bad batch of Botox, but as long as he throws touchdowns and commands late-game rallies people will look the other way at his immoral antics. Success erases the memory of an asshole's detractors.

THE 'HOLE TRUTH

The athlete asshole should not be confused with the recreational douche bag. These fellas populate beer-league sports teams but act as if they are getting paid to play. They deserve nothing but a loaded bat to the kneecaps for taking a fun weekend activity way too seriously.

The Musical Asshole

This asshole learned at a young age that mastering a musical instrument is the key to success in life and love. He probably hesitated at first, pissing and moaning every time he had to practice while his friends lit fire to G.I. Joes and fed the neighborhood cat packs of Big League Chew. But who's laughing now? This asshole can charm women with the strum of a guitar or thump of a drum and might actually make a living as a paid musician. Even a side gig in a cover band gets this asshole more attention than the typical bar crawler.

His Secret

People, especially women, love musical. The musician asshole has won tons of fans and admirers through his ability to play an instrument. People assume that as a musician he is deep and philosophical. That's bull; this asshole only knows how to pluck some strings. However, since the plucking sounds a little better than your armpit rendition of Blues Traveler's "Runaround," he gets the girl and you get a rash.

What You Can Learn

The obvious answer is a musical instrument. It's never too late to learn. The not-so-obvious lesson is that if you practice hard enough at one thing it can open more doors than you imagined. Assuming you go for the obvious and pick up an instrument, try the harmonica. It will work well for a solid version of "Runaround," help you get the girl, and avoid a rash (as long as you're smart about which girl you choose).

The Local-Celebrity Asshole

These guys aren't super famous like their Hollywood counterparts, but they still reap the benefits of having a recognizable face and public interest in their lives, even if it is only in a twenty-mile radius. Guys like the town athlete who received a standing-O on the high school field and made it into the minors or the pretty-boy prom king who had a three-second spot in a fast-food commercial. These are the guys who can parlay their fifteen seconds of fame into an eternity of local attention and perks by banking on their "celebrity" and likeability.

THE 'HOLE TRUTH

You're probably thinking, "What kind of celebrities **aren't** *assholes?" but that isn't necessarily true. Most are douche bags.*

His Secret

This asshole acts like he belongs everywhere and that everyone should be happy to have him around.

What You Can Learn

Get famous for anything. It doesn't even have to be a positive reason—infamous assholes can lead as fun a life as the celebrated local celebrity. Make a name and live off that name for as long as possible.

ASSHOLE IN ACTION: Charlie

Charlie was the undisputed asshole on campus in his prime. After graduation, he occasionally returned for homecoming and tailgating. One year, after an overtime win that saw the entire stadium stay until the final seconds, cars lined up for days in the parking lot going out one of the few exits. Not one to wait, Charlie piled everyone into his car and tore off down a one-way street—going the wrong way.

A police officer quickly stepped in front of his car and demanded he stop. Charlie, not one to back down from a fight, laid on the horn and screamed out the driver's window, "This happens every goddamn year!! If you pricks would let us leave out every possible direction this place would clear out and we'd be on our way! Now get the hell out of the way so we can get this traffic moving!"

Dumbfounded, the cop stared at Charlie, at a loss for words. The cop started laughing, stepped out of the way of the car, and waved him down the one-way street going the wrong direction.

The Single Asshole

He dates tons of women, sleeps with all of them, and never commits, yet comes off looking like the greatest guy in the world. Your female friends have probably dated him—you might even have been the one to set them up—but they don't hate him. This asshole manages to bed and befriend (and bed again) tons of attractive women. He's the chronic bachelor who's never actually alone, as he still hangs out with his conquests, meeting up for the occasional drink and screw.

His Secret

He's honest. He's up front. He lays it out for the ladies. This is what he is looking for and this is what they can expect. They have no one to blame but themselves for getting involved and choosing to ignore the asshole's warnings.

What You Can Learn

An asshole is honest. Be honest with women; it's an odd but effective approach.

Make It Work for You

Acting like an asshole will improve every facet of your life, but the three most important areas are covered in the following chapters—on the job, in social situations, and with the opposite sex. Ask yourself:

Could I do better at work?
Could I have more fun in life?
Could I be getting more ass?

You should've said yes to all three because no matter how powerful, carefree, or knee-deep in nookie you are, you can be deeper, happier, and more powerful.

It's possible to learn from each of the asshole archetypes and create a persona fit to your particular situation. You do not have any limits, only your own limitations. Now that's deep.

CHAPTER RECAP: What Type of Asshole Are You?

In order to establish your presence as an asshole, you have to find your niche and work it. There are many different types of assholes, and it's important you adopt an asshole persona that works with your talents. The more natural the attitude feels, the easier it will be to perfect. By working your niche, you'll be able to exploit the inherent advantages that come with the asshole role you fill. However, don't feel trapped by a single label. You can combine different asshole archetypes to create a hybrid that's all your own.

Ass • hole • ol • o • gy Vocabulary

Loophole (n.): An asshole's means of getting what he wants without dealing with any of the bullshit

Asshole detractor (n.): A person who hates on an asshole's game; typically synonymous with "douche bag"

Bed and befriend (v.): To sleep with a woman while establishing a connection that will lead to further hook ups

Character Study

The Social Asshole: He is a great specimen to study during your training process, as you will find him in the asshole's natural habitat: the watering hole. Watch as he moves effortlessly from group of people to group of people, nonchalantly taking control of every conversation he enters. Take note of his skills at recalling small details in order to network and establish his likability.

Questions to Think About
- What type of asshole do you most closely relate to? Why?
- How would you handle an asshole detractor?
- What is your niche?

What You *Should* Have Learned
- ❑ It's all about finding your niche.
- ❑ There are several different types of assholes. Learn about and from them.
- ❑ Uncle Al had hip surgery. Call him.
- ❑ Success erases the memory of an asshole's detractors.
- ❑ You have to shape your own asshole attitude.

Chapter 5
Act like an Asshole

Did you ever despise a person you barely knew? Something about him just rubbed you the wrong way. You couldn't put your finger on it, but there was something there. The way he looked. The way he spoke. The way he acted in public. Even his smell was off. He did things differently than you and it wasn't to your liking.

Here is the reason why: He was an asshole who was doing everything correctly while you're an idiot doing everything wrong: The way you dress. The way you speak. The way you act. Wrong, all wrong.

It's never too late to change, though. It does take time, effort, research, and a little cash, but it will pay off in the end. Ready to make the investment?

It's never too late to change.

Look like an Asshole

Buying the right clothes and looking your best isn't impossible. While some men act like it's as hard as splitting the atom or finding a virgin (both overrated once accomplished), it's not. The hard part is figuring out what looks good on you. For this, it's best to get someone else's opinion. Ask a female friend if she'd like to tag along. She'll be in the car planning your makeover before you can finish the sentence "I'm running to the mall. . . ." If you can't get a friend onboard, ask the opinion of the sales staff. This might be the better of the two options, as this person's taking an unbiased look at your new style.

THE 'HOLE TRUTH

If you don't trust the person at the store or even your friend, don't be afraid to get a few more opinions. Opinions are like assholes— everyone has one. (You knew that was going to be in here eventually.)

Size It Up

Once you've found a style that works for you—if it includes Ed Hardy T-shirts, keep looking—remember that size matters. Your clothes shouldn't be hanging off your body like those of a '90s hip-hop act. They also shouldn't be tight enough to cut off circulation. Choosing clothes that compliment your body type will make you look better. For a more thorough look into selecting the right cuts, pick up a book like *Esquire*'s *The Handbook of Style*. It'll do your closet good.

Tips to Dress By

Here are a few other quick tips to keep in mind:

- It's better to be overdressed than underdressed for any occasion.
- Don't be afraid to spend money. Good clothes are expensive, but cheap pieces end up costing more, as you have to keep buying replacements.
- Have at least one nice suit and one nice sport coat.

- There is never an appropriate occasion for a funny shirt.
- The best example of a good dresser is the store mannequin.
- Spend a little time keeping up on fashion, but don't be a victim to trends.

Learning how to dress is a slow process. You will know you're doing it correctly when you start to get compliments on the way you dress. Though laughing at your "clever" T-shirt is *not* a compliment.

You're dressing correctly when you start getting compliments.

DOUCHE BAG'S CLOSET

Here's what you can find hanging up in just about any douche bag's closet. (If you can also check off an item, time to throw it out.)

- ☑ Ed Hardy T-shirt
- ☑ Camouflage pants
- ☑ Visor
- ☑ Pink polo with starched and popped collar
- ☑ Store-bought ripped-and-stained jeans

Talk like an Asshole

An asshole has a certain way of commanding the English language. It's as much what he says as how he says it. The way he speaks is his tool to get what he wants, when he wants it. Every successful asshole must:

#1. Use Buzzwords

Buzzwords are crucial to the asshole vernacular. It keeps them one step ahead of the average person and makes everyone involved in the conversation, meeting, or discussion think the asshole knows what he's talking about even if they didn't understand the word. Buzzwords give an asshole's comments value, justification, and gravitas, and they are the benchmark for a successful semantic mapping. (We have no idea what the hell that means either, but we bet you think we did.)

THE 'HOLE TRUTH

The second a buzzword is picked up by a mainstream media outlet, stop using it.

#2. Memorize Stats and Statistics

"There are three kinds of lies," said Mark Twain "lies, damned lies, and statistics." Nothing ends an argument faster than rifling off numbers and figures that no one else can verify and, more importantly, dispute.

It doesn't even matter if they are accurate or correct. According to a recent study, almost 70 percent of people believe statistics are an effective tool in gaining the upper hand in debates and disputes. See, it works.

#3. Never End with "Am I Right?"

There is nothing worse than a person that gives their opinion matter-of-factly but then ends it with a question searching for approval.

News flash: An asshole is always right (at least in his own mind). Don't seek the approval of others and don't open the topic up for discussion or debate. State the facts (as you see them) and end the discussion: "There isn't a man alive that wouldn't slip it in Kathie Lee Gifford if they had the chance." End of discussion. *Hey!* End of discussion.

An asshole is always right (at least in his own mind).

FIVE THINGS YOU SHOULD *NEVER* SAY
1. Crème fraîche
2. Color palette
3. My cat did the cutest thing.
4. Is this shirt me?
5. Diet starts Monday.

THE QUOTABLE ASSHOLE
"Just remember: It's not a lie if you believe it."—George Costanza, *Seinfeld*

Know Your Shit

An asshole must know something about everything and everything about something. Pick a topic: history, baseball, stocks, boating, turn-of-the-century bread making; it really doesn't matter what the something is, just choose a topic and be an expert. Know everything there is to know and always strive to learn more. Make it known you are an authority on the subject: "Well, if we want to learn anything from the current economic crisis and volatile stock market, we need look no further than the yeast drought of 1768. Did you know that 43 percent of the population invested their money in bread and ovens? It was considered the safest option." Worked again.

THE 'HOLE TRUTH

Bread is one of the oldest prepared foods and dates back to the Neolithic era. The band Bread made cheesy love songs and dates back as early as 1969. Both are tough to digest in large amounts.

Not only is it important to be able to speak knowledgeably on a subject at all times, you must also excel at a particular activity—golf, cooking, painting, or something else that is not easily mastered by the average douche bag. Take that chef Rocco as an example of how mastering a talent can take an average guy and turn him into a famous, wealthy, hot-chick-bagging asshole. Now don't you wish you took Grandma up on those cooking lessons?

An asshole must know something about everything and everything about something.

Talk the Talk

Assholes dominate every conversation. It's expected. They are also expected to quickly and smartly defend their opinions on myriad topics. An asshole should be ready to shoot straight from the hip and have an educated argument to support his stance on a subject. (Don't talk out of your ass.)

Assholes dominate every conversation. It's expected.

To cover your bases, it's best to really keep up with the following four topics, and be ready to speak about them confidently and coolly at the next heated happy-hour debate:

Topic #1: Current Events—You don't have to be a walking newspaper. Just make sure you know the gist of every major story in the news. This is even easier with the Internet. Hit your favorite news website and check the "Most E-mailed" and "Most Discussed" sections. Find out what other people are talking about and do a little homework on the topic.

Topic #2: Sports—When surrounded by a group of men in any situation, the conversation will naturally turn to sports. Every guy will regurgitate an opinion they heard on sports talk radio or pass off a joke they read on a blog as their own quip on the sports culture. Assholes give their own opinion on sports; douche bags repeat what they hear on *Pardon the Interruption*. If the guys start discussing a sport the asshole doesn't watch or follow, he offers a pointed comment to draw a laugh and change subjects. "Who do I like in the Stanley Cup finals? Whichever team will put an end to an incredibly drawn out hockey season."

Douche bags repeat what they hear on *Pardon the Interruption.*

Topic #3: Religion and Politics—People believe these two taboo topics should not be discussed at parties or in mixed company. Why? Because you might piss someone off if you have an opposing viewpoint. Well, tough. If they feel so strongly about something they should want to defend their opinions. And you should be at the ready to go on the offense and show them how poorly they play D.

THE 'HOLE TRUTH

If you could give two shits about either topic, make that known as well: "I'd love to talk to you about God, but I save the fairytales for my kids' bedtime stories." At least it will keep you from getting invited back to these lame parties.

Topic #4: Everything—We know, we know . . . we said there would only be four, but an asshole is *never* wishy-washy on *any* subject. An asshole has an opinion and gives it when asked. Does it have to be the popular opinion? Nope. Just have something to say on the matter that doesn't make you sound like a dumbass. When in doubt, go against the norm. It's fun to stir the pot.

The ability to hold a conversation is an important part of being an asshole, seeing as how he's usually the center of the conversation. So mastering these talking tips means you're on your way.

Walk the Walk

Like with anything, you better be **able to** put up or you better just shut up. An asshole has to be able to back up everything he's shooting out of his mouth. Whether you need to actually hold your own against a guy that takes offense to something you say or follow through on a promise you've made, you're putting yourself out there, so you better be prepared.

Beyond backing up whatever your mouth gets you into, an asshole should know how to . . .

You're putting yourself out there, so you better be prepared.

. . . make a drink. Buy a bartending guide and learn how to make a good cocktail. While you don't need to be some pretentious collector of aged scotch or a nose-up sommelier, you should know the basics when it comes to alcohol, like the difference between a single malt and a double malt, a merlot and a cabernet, a hoppy pale ale and a Mad Dog 40/40, and so on.

. . . perform CPR. Will you ever use it? Hopefully not, but if the situation did arise, you would be able to take control. You need to know how to save a life. You will be glad you spent that Saturday afternoon mouth-humping a rubber dummy and pumping its chest. You'll also be thankful you took that CPR class.

THE QUOTABLE ASSHOLE
"It's all about bucks, kid. The rest is conversation."—Gordon Gekko, *Wall Street*

. . . grease people. Not in a perverted way. An asshole knows how to get into places by handing out presidential passes to the people that matter—bouncers, maitre d's—anyone who can grant an asshole fast access to an exclusive place.

For Every Action . . .

Once in a while a person is going to take issue with your asshole approach and attitude. They will go out of their way to try and expose you as nothing more than a pompous, arrogant douche bag. They may even threaten physical violence. Don't take the bait. Play it cool; don't be the douche bag. If the confrontation escalates to the point where this other guy is willing to lower himself to a fistfight for the sake of saving face, he isn't worth the time. Simply raise your hands, give one last smirk, and walk away. Be the better, not bigger, asshole.

THE 'HOLE TRUTH

The guy's jealous. He wishes he had your ability to articulate his thoughts and keep a crowd captive and entertained. If you want to be an asshole though, you have to be ready for these types of reactions. (You are being an asshole, after all.) However, you need to retain the coolness, calmness, and confidence that are inherent to the asshole attitude.

FIVE PEOPLE YOU SHOULD *NEVER* BULLSHIT (*EVER*)

1. Your father
2. Your doctor
3. Your accountant
4. The law
5. Another asshole

CHAPTER RECAP: Act like an Asshole

Assholes know how to do it right. You on the other hand are probably doing it wrong. You need to change the way you look (and by change we mean care about). You need to be able to carry on a conversation. You need to know how to handle yourself in public. Being an asshole is all about looking, talking, and acting in a way that will make people want to be around you.

Ass • hole • ol • o • gy Vocabulary

Semantic mapping (n.): Again, we don't know what this is

Slip it in (v.): To have sexual intercourse

Give two shits (exp.): An expression used to convey one's indifference for a situation, as in "Right after I slipped it, she was talking about 'a relationship' when I could really give two shits"

Character Study

Rocco DiSpirito: Now this is an asshole who banked on his talent. And even though it's not a necessarily manly talent, he still parlayed his knowledge into a good life (read: money, fame, women). Chef, restaurateur, and television personality, DiSpirito's success illustrates that you need to be good at something—and damn good at it if you want to be as successful as him.

Questions to Think About
- What do you think is wrong with your style?
- What conversation topic will you know everything about? Why?
- How would you handle a potential fight?

What You *Should* Have Learned
❑ This process will involve changes to your inside and your outside.

❑ Make the necessary changes to look the part.

❑ Learn how to talk like an asshole by using stats, memorizing buzz words, and never asking if you are right—*know* you are right.

❑ An asshole should have an opinion on all sorts of topics like current events, sports, religion, politics, and, well, everything.

❑ There are certain things every asshole should know how to do. This is your cue to learn them.

❑ People are going to take issue with your asshole approach. Be prepared to handle the situation.

Chapter 6
The Asshole at Work

The corporate world is filled with assholes. Most are at the top of the food chain: owners, CEOs, decision makers, and the guys that get to be in the company commercials and brochures. Yet some are still working their way up the lower rungs—working angles, making moves, and positioning themselves for a run to the top while you worry about taking too much time for lunch.

If you want to succeed in any business sector, you need to learn that being an asshole is a necessity. The expression "It's not personal; it's just business" was probably coined by an asshole that just screwed over an associate to make a deal that sealed him a promotion. He was right. Being an asshole isn't personal—it's just business. Now let's get down to business.

Your First Day: Start from the Beginning

You're the new guy. No one likes or trusts the new guy. You already have a strike against you with your coworkers. They all dislike you for different reasons: To the older generation of staff with thirty years in the can, you are the younger, cheaper alternative that is going to push them one step closer to accepting a buyout and crying in their cars staring at their boxes of office belongings. To the younger, you are the newbie they are going to have to train to use the copier, find the bathroom, and log into e-mail like a three-year-old with a learning disorder. Since everyone is already predisposed to despise you, this is the perfect opportunity to start being an asshole.

Announce Your Presence

The first day of work is confusing and frustrating. Few people are helpful and everyone expects the new guy to make the effort to introduce himself. Do just that. Say hello to people in the halls and everyone in the cubicles around yours, and turn the accidental bathroom bump-ins into quick conversations. (Just wait until after they come out of the stall.)

Really make your presence known.

After everyone knows your name, really make your presence known. This next move is tricky, but if done correctly can set the tone for the rest of your time at the company.

1. Find a reason to get incredibly angry with a coworker for no good reason.
2. Make it personal. If they remove something from your desk or make a comment toward you in mixed company, lose your mind for a brief moment.
3. Seal it with a threat. In an angry tone and with near-psycho eye contact tell them it would be best if they never did whatever

small thing they did again. "Don't ever, *ever* touch my *Wall Street Journal*."

Crazy? It's beyond crazy. But would you ever cross a person that flips out on someone for touching their newspaper?

Don't Ask, Just Do

Instead of asking people how the copier works, where the restroom is, or how hard you can punch the soda machine for stealing your quarters without alerting security, figure it out on your own. Open doors, check open rooms, screw around with the phone system—teach yourself the ins and outs of the office. If you do something dumb like intercom the entire office or pee in a coat closet, you get to flash the "I'm the new guy" card and get out of jail free. It's their fault for not teaching you the ropes.

THE QUOTABLE ASSHOLE
"Victorious warriors win first and then go to war, while defeated warriors go to war first and then seek to win."
—Sun Tzu

Grill the Person Training You

Most companies will designate a coworker to act as your trainer. This is the perfect time to ask all the real questions you couldn't ask on the interview:

Who's really two faced?
Who are the real decision makers in the place?
Who's on the fast track to management?
Who should be avoided?
Who knows all the dirt?

Pump him or her for anything that will help you form alliances, make smart moves, and climb the corporate ladder. If they can't (or won't) answer your questions, hunt out the office gossip yourself and make friends.

> ### THE QUOTABLE ASSHOLE
> "Lunch is for wimps."—Gordon Gekko, *Wall Street*

The First Few Months: Make Your Move

You've learned how the wheels turn. You know the players. You know how to manipulate your boss, your coworkers, and even the ladies in Admin. It's time to make a decision: Is this a job you'd like to stick with for a few years? Do you see yourself commandeering a corner office and barking orders at the people that already make your workday a frustrating experience? If the answer is no, you should spend your days updating your resume and sending out feelers to get a new gig. If the answer is yes, it's time to start cutting ties and making moves.

> It's time to start cutting ties and making moves.

Ditching the Cofriends

The first asshole move is to eliminate the dead weight called "cofriends" who drag down your progress on the job. Cofriends are the people you became friendly with solely based on the working situation. Either you trained together, ate lunch at the same time, or just happened to strike up a conversation in the copier room. Besides working for the same business, you really have nothing else in common with these people. If either of you left the company, you'd never talk again. Some friendship.

The truth of the matter is these people are holding you down. Management sees the relationship. They've taken notice and probably feel somewhere down the line it could hinder your ability as a manager to make decisions if you shared a pack of Chuckles with the people you'd be bossing around. Stop being friends slowly. Eat lunch in the lunchroom less, cut back on the number of nonwork e-mails you send and respond to, and just avoid them around the office. However, make sure they see it as you being too busy and not being a prick; you don't need to make enemies. Maintain a casual friendship by always staying loosely in touch.

THE 'HOLE TRUTH

The only exception to this rule is if the person has a higher position or a greater influence throughout the company. Then by all means ask about his dumb kids or comment how her new frosted perm accentuates her overtanned leathery skin.

Get Involved

The asshole is always a part of every important project at work. This doesn't happen by accident; it takes some maneuvering and manipulating.

The asshole is always a part of every important project.

First, decide what projects are the most important to the company's bottom line. Are they looking to score a huge new client? Positioning to buy out a competitor? Attempting to put their name on the top of every urinal cake on the East Coast? (Seriously, what the hell do you do for a living?) Figure out the head of those projects and offer your assistance in any capacity. An asshole makes himself available. Offer suggestions to the project manager and work every angle possible to snag an invite to the meetings. If the project is a success, your name is connected in some capacity and you could be asked to join in the next step toward urinal-cake domination. If the project goes south, you weren't one of the leads so the blame is placed elsewhere.

An asshole makes himself available.

Another solid move is to take up smoking, just for the first few months. Become part of the smoking crew that goes outside. It's these little moments of smokers' delight that always bring forth the most venomous and juiciest gossip. Don't say much, just quietly puff away and take in all the inside information.

THE 'HOLE TRUTH

To seem legit, pick the toughest cigarettes possible. Newports work well, or Marlboro Reds if you really feel like being an asshole to your lungs. It will be easy to quit, promise.

Don't Call Him Boss

No one likes the guy that is buddies with the boss. Who cares? You aren't trying to win a popularity contest; you're trying to win a promotion. Your office isn't a place for you to give a shit about other people's perceptions of you (at least those people who don't matter). A little brown nosing never hurt anyone.

You aren't trying to win a popularity contest; you're trying to win a promotion.

You have to be careful, though. Successful brown nosing is a tricky business because the boss can always tell a genuine person from a total ass kisser. Therefore, act like your boss isn't your boss. Remember, he started the same place you did—at the bottom, wandering the halls looking for the bathroom and unable to retrieve his voicemail for months. Ask his opinion on business matters. Go to him for advice on clients, handling coworkers, and anything about work that he loves rambling on about for hours. That is your chance to build a rapport. Comment on the crap in his office or the portly kids in the picture on his desk that look like they sweat butter. Show him you aren't intimidated by his position.

Act like your boss isn't your boss.

THE ASSHOLE'S FAVORITE OFFICE PHRASES

What He Says	What He Means
"Let me get back to you on that."	"I have no idea; let me find out so I don't sound dumb."
"I want to get your input."	"I want your help and will probably take all the credit for your ideas."
"Keep me in the loop."	"I don't care but I'm pretending I do."
"It is what it is."	"I don't give a shit."
"I'm out of pocket."	"Leave me the fuck alone."

The Management Promotion:
So Long, Suckers

Congratulations. You've made it. (Nice office.) You probably think you can tone down the asshole approach because you've reached your goal. Good job, boss, two minutes in the chair and you've already made a colossal error in judgment. Now more than ever, your asshole skills will come into play. You've reached the top, but now you have to stay there.

> Now more than ever, your asshole skills will come into play.

Not only will you have to be an asshole to everyone on the payroll, you'll have to do so in face-to-face and group meetings. Being in a position of authority means a ton of meetings with your underlings, as well as those above you on the office food chain. In these meeting, it's imperative to let your asshole shine through.

If it's a one-on-one meeting, be sure to make your agenda obvious and what you want accomplished crystal clear. Spell it all out so there is no questioning, second-guessing, or opportunities for the underlings to do anything except what you've specifically requested. Stay on topic, on point, and keep it brief. The longer the meeting, the less the subordinates will take away.

> Stay on topic, on point, and keep it brief.

During group meetings, always be the asshole in charge. Once again, set the agenda and dominate the conversation. If the conversation careens off topic (as it always does), be the person to bring the focus back to the topic at hand. Make sure the group is attentive, productive, and gets their shit done.

Keep the Crew in Line

Meetings with groups of coworkers are excellent opportunities to flex your asshole abilities. They provide the perfect chance to prevent mutiny in the crew. A common tactic of the insecure douche bag would be to pick on the weakest of the group. Wrong. Assholes pick on the strongest. Show everyone you are in charge and not one to be screwed with under any circumstance. Picking on the defenseless only rallies the troops under the "boss is a douche bag" flag. Put the strongest in check and the rest of the crew stays in line. Just make sure you can handle the dogfight; you don't want him to make you look like a giant pussy in front of your entire staff.

> Douche bags pick on the weakest. Assholes pick on the strongest.

ASSHOLE IN ACTION: Darren

Darren noticed his staff sometimes got lazy. This was incredibly obvious during the summer. It was almost like a case seniori-tis—except they weren't graduating. The nicer the weather, the more people would call off work or come down with a mystery ailment overnight. It usually always happened on Fridays, when the office turned into a ghost town after lunch.

Then Darren had an idea.

Darren decided to make Friday's the most important day of the workweek. He scheduled every one-on-one sales meeting with his staff members for Friday afternoons. He would give Friday deadlines for all projects. He even sometimes waited until Friday morning to call afternoon meetings. He called a staff meeting and e-mailed an agenda for the Friday before Labor Day, at 4:00 P.M. in the afternoon.

The entire staff huddled in the conference room. Darren was absent. At 4:01 P.M. he called in to his assistant to put him on speakerphone in the conference room. He ran the meeting from his car on the way to the beach.

Office Interactions

Even if you cut ties with most of your cofriends, you'll still have a few confidants in the office. This is acceptable as long as the rules are clear.

The other people have to understand that work is work. You have to be an asshole to get things accomplished. Remember: It's nothing personal; it's only business. The people you still socialize with need to realize this fact. If you chew one of them out at a meeting for being a total moron, they need to realize that's your job. He was a moron. You are the manager. Therefore, you have to lay into him. Now, he might take it a little personally and not talk to you the next time you're at the coffee machine or respond to your e-mail about a run during lunch, but he'll get over it. And if he doesn't, he clearly doesn't have what it takes to hang with you. Chew him out at the next meeting just for the hell of it.

The people you're friends with in the office should know you're an asshole by now anyway. They accept that fact and choose to associate with you despite it. These are people you should keep close. Every successful asshole needs connections throughout his organization. They will help you down the road.

> # Work is work. You have to be an asshole to get things accomplished.

Handling Mutual Hate

The idea of being an asshole to someone you don't like seems simple in theory, but in actuality, it's harder to be an asshole to a coworker you don't like than one you do.

Here's why: If you act like an asshole with a coworker who knows you're an asshole and can roll with the punches, they are more likely to accept how you go about doing business. If you're an asshole to a coworker that already wishes you'd jam your hand into a bucket of rusty nails, then getting through to him on a business level will be near impossible.

The simple solution: Treat the people you hate (somewhat) better than the people you like. Even if you despise that guy in sales who sports more hair gel than Ryan Seacrest, you can't make it known throughout the ranks. Again, picking on him from a place of power simply because you don't like him is wrong. It will reduce morale as you come off looking petty, even if he comes off looking douche-y. You don't want the troops to know whom you hate, so keep everyone on their toes. As much as it might pain you, you occasionally have to throw the tool a bone in the form of a compliment—only when he deserves it, of course.

The Asshole Outside the Office

Common knowledge dictates that you rarely want to be in situations outside the office that will give coworkers an opportunity to get to know you on a personal level. Sometimes, however, it's unavoidable. You have to be careful in those instances. One too many shots of Cuervo and your asshole authority is out the window. Don't let that happen.

First, maintain the same relationship outside the office that you do within the poorly decorated walls. Don't be a prick. It is a social situation after all. Just remember that those under your command in the office should show the same respect at a bar or Christmas party. Be friendly but not chummy. Have a drink or two, make small talk, then say a quick goodbye and go home. You made the attempt to rub elbows with the common folk and did so in a civil manner. Plus, once you leave everyone can relax and have a few drinks. No one wants to drink with their boss.

Treat the people you hate (somewhat) better than the people you like.

Secondly, never, under any circumstance, make an appearance at an event that involves the family of a coworker. Unless the other person is an honest to Jesus real friend that you feel close enough to that you'd hit them up for an organ in case of emergency, don't get involved with coworkers lives outside the office. It's a slippery slope that will affect every decision you make during business hours. It would be hard to fire Ted under normal circumstances; imagine having to fire Ted after bringing bean dip to his BBQ and meeting his wife, kids, and one-eyed cat Mr. Handsome Pants. Personal relationships affect your ability to be an effective asshole on the job. Stay focused. Get Mr. Handsome Pants out of your mind.

CHAPTER RECAP: The Asshole at Work

Being an asshole isn't personal, it's just business—especially when it comes to work. In order to achieve your career goals by acting like an asshole, you need to make your presence known immediately. Make sure your officemates recognize that you're not just some pen pusher and you're not to be messed with. Get involved in the important projects so that you get noticed by the higher-ups and promoted. And once you do get that promotion: take no prisoners. Remember, it's business, nothing personal.

Ass • hole • ol • o • gy Vocabulary

Work an angle (v.): To persuade another person into doing something through cunning

Office gossip (n.): Trivial shit you would not care about outside the workplace, but prize because it's useful intellect inside your office

Cofriend (n.): A coworker with whom you are friendly

Character Study

The Office Gossip: Usually this person is not an asshole, but that does not mean there isn't something you can learn from him or her (usually women are seen as gossips, but inside an office all bets are off). They know everyone. They talk to everyone. They listen to everyone. They're a wealth of knowledge for you to dip into when the time is necessary.

Questions to Think About

- What role do you fill in your current job?
- What is your ultimate career goal?
- How will becoming an asshole help you to achieve your career goal?

What You *Should* Have Learned

- ❏ There are assholes at work. It's in your best interest to be one of those assholes.
- ❏ You should be an asshole on your first day.
- ❏ As you grow with the company, let your asshole persona grow as well.
- ❏ You have your friends and you have your coworkers. Know where to draw the line.
- ❏ It's usually harder to be an asshole to people you don't like than those you do.
- ❏ When you're the boss, no one really wants to see you at happy hour—but make an appearance anyway.

Chapter 7
The Asshole at Play

You can't just turn off being an asshole—it's not like there's a switch that lets you flip it on when you feel like it. If you commit to being an asshole, you have to be one every day, everywhere, in every aspect of your life. Whether you're watching football at a friend's house or walking down the aisle in a wedding party, an asshole is an asshole twenty-four hours a day, seven days a week.

The Asshole in Public

The asshole should always be the center of attention. No matter where he is or what he's doing, the asshole finds a way to be the person everyone wants to be around. There is, however, a fine line between commanding attention as an asshole and drawing attention as a douche bag. As your mother used to say, you want to be the person people laugh with, not the one they laugh at. So, here are some typical situations you'll find yourself in and the how-to for pulling off the perfect asshole behavior.

At a Bar

The watering hole is the asshole's playground. It's where friends are met, fun is had, and deals are done, for both business and pleasure. Even in the most crowded bar, an asshole can make his presence known without coming across as obnoxious. Here are some tips to help you step up your A-game the next time you head out to the bars.

> Even in the most crowded bar, an asshole can make his presence known without coming across as obnoxious.

TIP #1: GET CHUMMY WITH THE BARTENDER

It's a crucial, crucial move that must be mastered. The bartender is the most important person to get on your side on any trip to a gin joint. Get there early so it isn't too busy and start up a conversation. Always begin by asking the bartender's name. But don't start and end every sentence with it. You want to get in his or her good graces without trying too hard. And if the bartender is female, don't make it seem like a pick-up attempt. Keep it friendly; ask questions, especially about drinks. And this should go without saying, but tip and tip well. Every time.

Once the bar is three deep and everyone is fighting for the bartender's attention waving Andrew Jacksons in the air yelling "Hey!" and "Yo!" the bartender will be happy to hear a quick, "Jim, when you get a chance, another round please" from the friendly, familiar voice of an asshole. Getting in with the bartender will also help in case anything gets out of hand. If things go down and the bouncers want to know the whole story, they will usually ask the bartender what happened. So, if you're buddy-buddy with the bartender, chances are their recount will cast you in a favorable light.

Tip and tip well. Every time.

TIP #2: REMEMBER NAMES AND DRINKS

Recalling a person's drink of choice is almost as important as recalling that person's name. It's a personal touch to any encounter that every asshole should learn to pull off. Not only does getting it right for that night's next round help in the now, it's a great way to show off your attention to detail the next time you get together at a bar. If you can meet up with an acquaintance or business contact and order his favorite drink before he does, it shows you pay attention. And an asshole remembers even the smallest detail. Knowing he prefers soda water over tonic or his brand preference will make you ordering that Ketel One and soda even more remarkable.

An asshole remembers even the smallest detail.

FIVE DRINKS YOU SHOULD *NEVER* ORDER

1. **Margarita:** Unless you're a Mexican singer named El Pussy.
2. **Apple martini:** Martinis are for drinking; apples are for eating or picking. (P.S. *Never* go apple picking either.)
3. **Diet anything:** The only exception is if you mix it with alcohol harder than your crotch at a strip club.

4. **Sex on the beach:** Only actual sex on an actual beach is acceptable (though the sand trap on the 16th hole does count).

5. **Milk:** Put the book down. Run face first into a wall. Who told you to stop?

TIP #3: TALK TO THE CROWD

This is normally the first mistake in networking, meeting new people, or even picking up the opposite sex—don't start by talking to just one person in a crowd of people. This immediately alienates the rest of the group and puts the conversation on display. An asshole always engages a group with a broad, open-ended question. This involves everyone in the conversation and gets them familiar with the asshole. Once a connection is established, the asshole can focus his attention on a smaller set of people and strike up a conversation with one or two individuals.

Don't start by talking to just one person.

TIP #4: PEE NICE WITH OTHERS

Normally, the bathroom is the last place you'd expect to make friends. However, it's usually the quietest place in the bar. A well-timed joke while waiting for a urinal or while washing your hands is always a good way to win over the other gentlemen. Not only will it score you a few laughs then, you're now the funny guy if you run into any of them outside the restroom: "Hey, you were that guy who made the 'Where's the Drakkar?' joke at the sink." Yes, you were. (And you better have been joking.)

TIP #5: STOP PLAYING GAMES

Darts. Pool. Shuffleboard. All great ways to pass the time when it's just you and a few friends kicking back at the bar blowing off steam. However, if you're trying to meet new people, you should avoid playing bar games when you go out for the night; they limit your possibilities. Sure, you might make friends with the two or three people you're playing with, but you're losing valuable time making your presence known around the entire bar. When you're finally knocked off the table a few hours later, everyone's already involved in intoxicated talks that you're not going to be able to work your way into. Let the shy wallflowers and competitive d-bags run the table; you should be working on your real game.

And beyond these tips, the most important thing to remember is to be social. Always move around the bar. Talk to different people. Get involved in different conversations. Go be a social butterfly with a gin and tonic in hand.

At a Wedding

For the bride and groom, a wedding is the celebration of their love and their joining together in holy matrimony to live the rest of their lives as one and raise a family. For everyone else, it's an excuse to drink heavily, eat a lot, and have a ball on the couple's dime. It's also prime time to be an asshole. It's a great opportunity to catch up with friends and relatives, network with new people, and possibly get your whistle wet with an available woman. Like in the bar, it's all making your presence known.

It's all about making your presence known.

First, get to know everyone at the ceremony. Build a connection. Talk to everyone and let them know who you are and why you're attending the wedding.

"The bride and I grew up together."
"The groom and I work together."
"I used to knock boots with the bride in college."

Carry on that conversation at the cocktail hour. Ask a million questions. Remember how they are connected to the happy couple as well as a few random details about their relationship.

When it comes time to get your grub on, make friends with your table if you're seated with strangers. Introduce yourself and keep everyone involved in the conversation. Avoid awkward silences by commenting on the couple, the food, or the venue to get the whole table talking. This makes the entire evening much more enjoyable. It also ensures those guests will walk away from dinner remembering how you kept everyone entertained.

THE QUOTABLE ASSHOLE

"We are gonna have tons and tons of opportunities to meet gorgeous ladies that get so aroused by the thought of marriage that they'll throw their inhibitions to the wind."
—Jeremy Grey, *Wedding Crashers*

Once dinner's over and the night moves on to dancing and more drinks, try and locate the people you found most important in your earlier mingling—the doctor with a membership to that exclusive course, the bride's cousin with season tickets, the woman who doesn't want to be at a wedding since she's newly single. Now's the chance to get the return on the time you invested earlier. Recall those pieces of information that may have seemed useless, but that brought up in conversation now will show how attentive, detail oriented, and considerate you are.

And once you're done with this stage of the networking, be sure to open the door for a nonwedding follow up: "Hey, if I don't see you the rest of the night, give me your card or e-mail and we can meet up." So now, with the networking out of the way, you're allowed to really enjoy the party. However, it's important not to take too much attention away from the bride and groom. You aren't there to ruin their wedding. Keep in mind: You are a terrible dancer; don't let the vodka fool you.

THE 'HOLE TRUTH

Employ the same drink-memorization skill that you picked up in the bar section. After dinner, circle back to someone you met during the cocktail hour and ask them if they need a refill: "Can I get you another Jack and ginger?" Then, go grab a drink for yourself and what's his name.

At a Funeral

No one *wants* to be at a funeral (hell, even the guest of honor isn't thrilled to be in attendance), but we all have to attend funerals every now and then. Be careful though: An improperly trained asshole can get in a shitload of trouble if he isn't careful.

When you go to pay your respects to the dead, be sure to give your regrets to the family and sign the guest book. Don't try to be clever in what you sign; be solemn and appropriate. Then go and hang in the back of the room. It's where people go to talk. Take the same approach with going around and greeting people as you would at a wedding, except be a little more reserved. Also, don't offer to get any drinks. Unless it's an Irish wake. Out of respect for the dead, this is as far as we will go into funeral networking.

THE QUOTABLE ASSHOLE
"I'm very sorry for your loss. Your mother was a terribly attractive woman."—Royal Tenenbaum. *The Royal Tenenbaums*

At Dinner

A group of friends are getting together to chow down, shoot the shit, and enjoy each other's company over tasty fare and several bottles of wine. It's not really that intimate since the restaurant is packed with groups and couples doing the same. How does the asshole act? As if he is the person throwing the dinner. Follow these steps to secure your place as the asshole host.

1. Sit at the head of the table. This is where everyone will be looking, and will announce you as the leader of the group. If they seat your party at a round table, sit on the side that faces the rest of the restaurant. Now you can see everyone and everyone can see you.

2. Become the waiter's go-to guy. Start by being the one who orders something for the whole table—be it an appetizer or a bottle of wine—show him you're the one calling the shots. Now, when he has any questions or needs to break the news that they're all out of salmon, he'll come to you.

THE 'HOLE TRUTH

As the asshole leader, your food will get screwed with first if you have any douche bags in your dinner party. This gig isn't all roses and hand jobs.

---

3. At all times, try and speak for the crowd—order more bread, more drinks, be the one to ask for the dessert, and so on.

4. Take charge when it's time to pay. The waiter will likely place the bill closest to you since you've been the point person all night. When it comes to divvying up the damage, suggest the democratic approach to split the bill evenly. If that gets shot down, make sure to be the money collector; it's your job to make sure everyone pays what they owe.

5. Once everything's been figured out, hand the server the bill with your payment slips and cash. Make sure he gets the tip and thank him for a wonderful meal.

While you didn't lift a finger to put the meal together, everyone will leave thinking it was your dinner. Well done.

The Asshole in Private

When an asshole attends a gathering of family and friends it's one of the rare opportunities for him to let his guard down. He already knows everyone there and they all know him; therefore, he doesn't have to introduce himself to random strangers. However, it doesn't mean he can just forget about being an asshole. While he doesn't have to spend time making introductions, he does have to work the room. Here's a breakdown of some typical events that you'll undoubtedly have to attend, and how you can pull off being the best asshole you can be.

Family Gatherings

The asshole of the family is the guy who all the other members enjoy being around during the holidays. His birthday's never forgotten, he always gets a Christmas card, and everyone is hesitant about going on the big family vacation until he commits. However, he has to work to achieve that status.

The only way to survive these family get-togethers is with laughs and liquor.

Family gatherings are the perfect venue to begin your reign as your family's asshole. Make your way around the party, stopping to catch up with everyone. The quicker you move from person to person the more everyone else will want to talk to you. Drop some jokes, make fun of your uncle's golf game, be the person who gets everyone laughing—at other family members. The only way to survive these family get-togethers is with laughs and liquor. Bring a bottle for the host and get everyone going about how bad your aunt is at cooking.

Dinner Parties

These intimate gatherings are the perfect opportunity to sharpen your asshole skills, as you're among friends. Because who else can you piss off without serious retaliation if not the guy who puked in your sink a couple New Year's Eves ago?

Be sure to counter the one-liners and digs you'll be playfully shooting off during dinner with an expensive bottle of wine or the host's preferred alcohol as your thanks for the invite. Keep everyone entertained during dinner with an embarrassing little round of "Remember when . . ." (though stories like the New Year's Eve booting session are better suited for after dinner). And then impress the table by flexing your mind muscles, dazzling the crowd with your knowledge of myriad topics, which you've become an expert on—at least enough to offer a stat and an opinion.

After dinner, be the first to compliment the host for putting together such a nice get-together, but don't be afraid to throw in a few zingers, as you can't turn into a complete softy. Once everyone's finished the first round of after-dinner drinks, be ready to make your exit. You don't want to be the first one to leave, but you also don't want to be the last.

Birthdays and Other Special Occasions

Only an asshole can attend a birthday party for someone else and find himself the center of attention. How does an asshole accomplish such a feat? By being overly attentive to the person whose birthday it is—make an impromptu speech in his or her honor, buy the biggest gift, or just go out of your way to be around the guest of honor. The asshole doesn't save this type of behavior for just birthdays, though—going-away parties, bachelor parties, graduations—it doesn't matter the reason for celebration. As long as it's in honor of one person, the asshole has someone to overshadow.

CHAPTER RECAP: The Asshole at Play

An asshole is an asshole twenty-four hours a day, seven days a week. You need to stay on top of your game and focus on the details and never let your guard or attitude slip. Whether you're at a bar or at a funeral, you need to play the role of the asshole. Granted, the behavior in each situation does vary, but your ultimate goal remains the same: build connections and be remembered. You want people to know who you are. And you want them to want to be around you.

Ass • hole • ol • o • gy Vocabulary

A-game (n.): The best you have to offer, which better be better than everyone else in the room

Wallflower (n.): A shy person who stands by and lets life pass him by

Roses and hand jobs (exp.): Sweet rewards

Character Study

The Laughed-at Douche Bag: As an asshole, you want to be laughed with—not laughed at. Therefore, the Laughed-at Douche Bag is an important person to study. Notice how hard he tries. It should never look like you're trying. Your attitude and actions should come off as natural (that's where the practice comes into play). You should also never go after easy targets. No one really wants to laugh at those types of jokes. Why pick on a wallflower when you can make fun of a douche bag?

Questions to Think About
- Do people mostly laugh with you or at you?
- How will you change your approach at the bar?
- In what types of situations do you play the wallflower? How can that be fixed?

What You *Should* Have Learned
- ❑ Memorizing movies isn't really a good life skill.
- ❑ Assholes never take the day off.
- ❑ Even in a relaxed social situation, the asshole should be on his game.
- ❑ Master the art of being an asshole in public and in private.
- ❑ Assholes are always the center of attention.

Chapter 8
The Asshole and the Opposite Sex

You've heard the expression time and time again: Women love assholes. It's true. In fact, many of the world's most storied lovers have had immeasurable asshole qualities. Don Juan, considered one of the greatest lovers the world has ever known, took immense pleasure in seducing spoken-for women and then fighting the men in their lives for that love. Romeo, the model of young love and romance, falls for the daughter of the head of a rival family even though he knows it will land him in deep shit. John Mayer, singer and modern-day lothario, has bedded some of the world's most sought-after A-list celebrities, only to break their hearts via Twitter and TMZ.

NOTCHES ON JOHN MAYER'S BEDPOST
- ☑ Jessica Simpson
- ☑ Jennifer Aniston
- ☑ Jennifer Love Hewitt
- ☑ Your mom

Women don't just date assholes because of a physical attraction; women date assholes because these men aren't afraid to make an impression and then make a move. An asshole isn't too intimidated to talk to the hottest woman in the room. If he gets shot down, so be it; at least he tried. Hit on enough gorgeous women (or any women at all) and the asshole is bound to find success.

An asshole isn't too intimidated to talk to the hottest woman in the room.

How the Asshole Gets the Girl

Think about every time (or that one time) you successfully picked up a girl. Each instance has one thing in common: She was drunk. Kidding. They all occurred because the opportunity presented itself: The woman in the grocery store who reached for the same box of Cap'n Crunch; the girl in the elevator who hit your floor's button just as you were about to; the new office assistant who needed help with unjamming the copier. You only got up the nerve to start a conversation because of a little dumb luck.

Assholes don't wait.

Now here is the difference between your wait-and-see approach and the mark of a genuine asshole: Assholes don't wait. Assholes make their own openings and opportunities. While you've been hoping the new girl in the apartment above yours will be at the mailbox at the same time as you, the asshole down the hall already knocked on her door, welcomed her to the building, and has been busy charming his way into her bedroom. All while you idled in the lobby waiting for Mr. Postman to deliver your next issue of *Cat Fancy*. He got the girl; you got step-by-step instructions on how to knit your own kitten mittens.

FIVE WOMEN YOU SHOULD *NEVER* HIT ON
1. Best friend's mom
2. Girlfriend's mom
3. Girlfriend's sister
4. Cousin (blood or no blood relation)
5. Boss's wife (unless he is a douche)

In order to score like an asshole you have to act like an asshole. The three most important asshole intangibles to assume when approaching a woman are confidence, experience, and calculated luck.

Confidence

An asshole needs an incredible amount of confidence in any situation, especially when dealing with the opposite sex. An asshole fears nothing. He especially doesn't fear the word "no." An asshole probably hears that word almost twice as much as he hears the word "yes"; yet he doesn't cower in the corner when it's tossed his way. He brushes it off and hits on an even hotter girl.

Experience

Would you fly a plane without taking lessons? Give a presentation in front of your boss without doing extensive research? Go into your fantasy draft without reviewing last season's stats? Then why would you dare attempt to bed incredibly attractive females without trying your hand at every single girl you meet. All females are considered target practice—young, old, emaciated, portly, crazy, hell, even *Twilight* fans (as long as they're legal). The asshole doesn't discriminate until it's actually time to choose a woman to ask out.

Calculated Luck

Chance. Coincidence. Dumb luck. That's what the old you would rely on to start a conversation. Assholes can't be bothered by events out of their control; an asshole makes his own luck. Sometimes it looks like things just fall into his lap. A chance encounter, a random meeting, or being in the right place at the right time. But do you really think he brought all those extra quarters to the laundromat by accident? That the bartender really mixed up his Scotch on the rocks with a pomegranate mojito? That his run in with the hot chick from accounting really was random even though it was at the Starbucks around the block where she goes every morning at 10:45? Didn't think so.

An asshole makes his own luck.

ASSHOLE IN ACTION: Nick

Nick waited for the ATM to spit out what little money he had in his checking account. At least he could have a good time at the bar that night and worry about his finances in the morning.

Waiting for the machine to spit out his measly $20, Nick nosed around in the pile of other ATM slips that people had left behind after their transaction. One of the slips showed a checking account balance of $20,000. Nick was amazed both at the thought of having that much money in a checking account and that someone would carelessly leave information like that in public view.

Then he had a brilliant idea. He slipped the transaction receipt in his pocket. Later that night at the bar, after talking to a cute girl for much longer than his friends claim he should have, Nick took the slip of paper out his pocket and wrote his name and number on the opposite side of the balance.

"Do you really think a chick is going to call you?" his friends laughed, busting Nick's balls at the diner after last call.

She called the next day.

THE QUOTABLE ASSHOLE
"You're rather attractive for a beautiful girl with a great body."—Ty Webb, *Caddyshack*

The Asshole Approach

If you see a woman that piques your interest or just looks like a fun ride, here are two typical asshole strategies to make the initial contact much less painful for the both of you:

Be prepared.

Be a Boy Scout

No, don't dress in tight culottes and practice your knotting; be prepared. Have several topics at your disposal to get the conversation started and keep it moving. For example, if your supermarket is stocked to the shelves with gorgeous women, have a question and anecdote ready: "Do you have any idea where they keep the paprika around here? I'm making a Hungarian chicken for dinner and it's a major component. Have you ever had a Hungarian chicken?"

THE 'HOLE TRUTH

If you're going to pull this off, actually know a little something about your topic other than superficial facts. Suppose she is a Hungarian sous chef? Now what, Emeril?

Be a Clown

Ask a woman the most attractive feature in a man, and they will most likely reply, "A sense of humor." What is the best target for jest? Her. It sounds like a kamikaze mission, but lightly poking fun at a woman actually works. If you are funny, charming, and a bit of a wiseass, her guard drops quicker than Lindsey Lohan's pants without a belt. She will laugh at herself.

Let's take the supermarket example again. Once you've struck up a conversation, poke fun at some of her product choices: "I can see you wouldn't have time to prepare Hungarian chicken when you've got all this Cap'n Crunch to finish."

THE 'HOLE TRUTH

There is a fine line between making a few funny remarks and being a douche. Not sure if you've crossed the line? Ask the arresting officer.

If this situation scares the dollar-store boxers off your balls, just remember that asking questions allows her to do most of the talking. There is nothing a woman loves more than talking about herself. Make the questions general and not too specific. Save the grilling for the first date.

ASSHOLE IN ACTION: David

David loves to talk on his cell phone even when he really isn't on the phone. He especially loves to do this in front of attractive women.

Every afternoon, during his lunch hour, he stands in front of the door to his office building and makes his phantom phone calls. The more attractive the woman, the more important the phone conversation: million-dollar deals, purchasing brand-new sports cars, and even signing off on a lease for a beach house for the entire summer. The closer they get, the louder he speaks into the phone.

It doesn't always work at picking up a woman at that exact moment, but it helps to plant a seed. All of these women work in the building. They will recognize his face when he says hello in the parking garage or on the elevator up to their floor. The women will at least be mildly interested.

What happens when a woman finds out he is an administrative assistant who doesn't have a brand new car or a beach house is an issue for another time.

The First Date

This is where you establish just what type of relationship could come from this uncomfortable small talk and overpriced food. You better bring your A-game. An asshole takes control from the get-go; he chooses the time, the place, and all of the events for the evening. If she doesn't like the choices, she can fake it and pretend she is having the time of her life. What's important is being decisive; women want a man who can make decisions.

An asshole takes control from the get-go.

Keep the conversation going by asking her questions about her life. Imagine this is a job interview and she is applying for a position (if she does well it could lead to a ton of other positions, most involving her body bent like a silly straw). Use this as a time to find out everything about her.

By the end of dinner, you should have already made your decision about the future of this relationship. An asshole places his first date into one of three categories:

A. **Ms. Right-for-Now:** She isn't the future, but she is a good woman with a head on her shoulders, two balloons on her chest, and is willing to roll with the punches. She has potential and is worth getting to know past this first encounter.
B. **Ms. Right-Between-the-Legs:** She isn't girlfriend material, but that doesn't mean you can't have a little fun.
C. **Ms. Right-out-the-Door:** As in, cut your losses, call it a night, and go your separate ways right out of the door of the restaurant. She isn't worth a relationship or even a quick ball brushing against her Brillo pad.

If she falls into one of the first two categories, here is how to handle the rest of the evening. (If she falls into the last one, pull the ripcord and parachute out of this nose-diving plane ride.)

With Ms. Right-for-Now . . . act natural, interested, but somewhat aloof. Keep her guessing. An asshole never shows his hand. You can continue the date with a drink or two, but stay in control of the situation. A simple kiss on the cheek and a "Call you soon" should end the evening. Wait a day and give her a call. Don't listen to the other bullshit rules. Assholes call promptly and set up a second date.

An asshole never shows his hand.

With Ms. Right-Between-the-Legs . . . make your intentions known, but with a quick change of control. Make her seem like the aggressor. Accuse her of trying to get you drunk, attempting to get in your pants, and making inappropriate sexual suggestions. Play the poor, innocent guy who isn't looking for a just a quick dick-dunk. Do it well, and in a few hours you'll be bumping uglies at her place.

An Asshole in a Relationship

Any good relationship is a give and take; the asshole gives his thoughts on how things will work and his partner usually just takes it. Fine, it's not that simple, but an asshole usually does mold the relationship according to his own preferences. It sounds like a douche move, but a woman would do the same thing if she had the chance. In every relationship, there is a dominant partner. The asshole is always dominant.

THE QUOTABLE ASSHOLE

"The only reason to wait a month for sex is if she's seventeen years, eleven months old."—Barney Stinson, *How I Met Your Mother*

How does an asshole impose his will on his partner without coming off like a douche? It's all in the presentation.

Set the groundwork early. Make it known from day one that this is the way you want things to work. You hold the remote. You pick the restaurant. You introduce a new partner in the bedroom. (Fuck it—she went for everything else. Worth a shot, right?) She will have more than enough time to get out of dodge. If she is fine with the situation, she is a keeper. She also might not speak English. (You did meet in a loud bar.)

Voice your displeasure. She changed the channel during a TV timeout? She picked up Chinese food for dinner from that take-out place you hate? She invited Victor over for drinks and a possible threesome without asking your opinion? It doesn't matter how handsome Victor is with his chiseled cheekbones and smell of cured meat—snap out it! Get fired up. Tell her you are unhappy with the situation. Ask her to respect your wishes. Express your asshole feelings. Ask Victor to come back Sunday after mass.

THE 'HOLE TRUTH

This is probably one of the few times an asshole is allowed to express his emotions, so try and get as much off your chest as possible (i.e. her nosey mother).

Bend; don't break. It's fine to ease up if you actually like this woman, but don't let go of all your rules. It's a pretty cool trick if you can pull it off. Give in to some small stuff; make her think she is getting what she wants. It's an asshole's way of staying in complete control. She really isn't making any decisions at all. Goddamn it, Victor, go home!

Give in to some small stuff; make her think she is getting what she wants.

The Asshole and the Breakup

Breakups are never easy. However, this is where the asshole really separates from the douche bag. Ever notice that most assholes are always still friendly with ex-girlfriends? Ever notice assholes usually continue to hook up with their exes long after the relationship has ended?

A true asshole is honest to a fault.

Be a Man

Even if you don't care very much for the woman, being a man about the situation will go a long way in maintaining your reputation, and the foundation of a quality booty call. Always break things off with a face-to-face encounter. She deserves the respect and the chance to express her feelings about the situation. Don't shoot her an e-mail or late-night text. Most importantly, don't pull the disappearing act and never call her again. A true asshole is honest to a fault. Tell her exactly why you feel things didn't work out, even if it was all her fault. You could be teaching her things about herself that she is unaware of and saving her from other heartbreaks down the road.

THE 'HOLE TRUTH

If she doesn't pick up or return the call, just let it go. Don't try to be the nice guy by attempting to remain friends; it might be best to lose contact. Also, think about a name change because some shit could be ready to go down. Do you have a will?

Once the deal has been done, give it a few days and check up on her with a quick phone call or e-mail. Tell her you were thinking about her and wanted to say hello. Keep it friendly, never flirty, and leave on a good note.

FIVE THINGS YOU SHOULD FORGET (FOR YOUR OWN GOOD)

1. **The number of women you have slept with**—knowing this exact number will never come in handy. Not even if you make it on *Jeopardy!*

2. **A bitter ex's phone number**—there's a reason she is a reason she is bitter. Don't revisit it.

3. **Your last round of golf**—it doesn't mean shit this round.

4. **The first girl that turned you down**—it's all water under the bridge. Get over it. Also, we've seen her, and she is the size of said bridge.

5. **The mistakes of the past**—you'll be making many more in the future. Let them go.

THE QUOTABLE ASSHOLE

"What you call love was invented by guys like me to sell nylons."—Don Draper. *Mad Men*

Assholes and Love

Assholes aren't heartless beings; they have feelings and emotions just like everyone else. They emit the same salty wet discharge from their eyes just like a normal human. An asshole can fall in love. An asshole can also have his heart broken. (There's even a good chance that the broken heart led to his asshole behavior. Yes, your mind was just blown.)

Assholes aren't heartless beings; they have feelings and emotions just like everyone else.

However, assholes don't let love get in the way of their true nature. Even though an asshole's as susceptible to the pinprick of Cupid's arrow as your typical Mr. Nice Guy, he knows how to bench that diaper-sporting, flying imp in order to keep his eyes on the prize. Because while assholes may be able to fall in love, there's a more important truth: Women love assholes. And assholes love tapping any women that are in love with them as much as they are in love with themselves.

CHAPTER RECAP: The Asshole and the Opposite Sex

Women love assholes. An asshole isn't afraid to make a move, which leaves a lasting impression with the ladies (hopefully a good one). Therefore you need to try. You're only going to attain success by risking failure. What you need to be an asshole with the opposite sex is confidence, experience, and calculated luck. Don't leave things up to chance. And when you do find that girl, be sure to play an active role in the relationship. And when you do break up with her, be sure to remain friends so you have an easy booty call during your search for Ms. Right.

Ass • hole • ol • o • gy Vocabulary

Lothario (n.): A man skilled in the art of seduction

Calculated luck (n.): The process of taking the necessary actions to secure a desired outcome

A ball-brushing against her Brillo pad (exp.): Sexual intercourse

Character Study

John Mayer: This guy oscillates between being an a-hole and being a d-bag almost hourly. However, he's having a fun time doing it. Mayer subscribes to working your niche as described in Chapter 4. He plays the role of Musical Asshole perfectly, and has reaped its bountiful benefits (see: Jennifer Aniston). A singer/song-writer from Connecticut, Mayer's musical fingers have allowed him to touch some of the most beautiful bodies in the world. Hats off to you Mr. Mayer. Douche bag or not.

Questions to Think About

- Why do you always strike out at the bar?
- How do you plan on using calculated luck?
- How did you handle your last breakup? How would being an asshole have made it different?

What You *Should* Have Learned

- ❑ Assholes usually get the girl.
- ❑ Getting a woman is a combination of confidence, experience, and calculated luck.
- ❑ Decide what you want from a relationship as soon as possible. It saves everyone involved time and feelings.
- ❑ Assholes should explain what they want out of relationship from the beginning.
- ❑ Assholes should handle a breakup with as much class as possible.
- ❑ Assholes can fall in love. (Isn't that romantic.)

Part III
The Aftermath

Chapter 9
You're an Asshole . . .
Now What?

If you made it this far, you should be incredibly proud. Those extra reading classes have really paid off. You should also pat yourself on the back for being an incredible asshole. While it's likely the only person actually voicing his admiration for your new attitude is, well, you, people *will* notice the difference. However, they may not always appreciate that difference. So, here's the best way to handle your critics: Don't give a fuck. Why should you? Life is too short to try to please everyone.

Now that you've attained asshole status, there are a few things to keep in mind.

#1. ALWAYS KEEP A LEVEL HEAD.

Sure life is great right now, but things can and will go wrong. Life isn't perfect; it's going to have its ups and downs like before, except the downs won't knock you that far and the ups will only make you hunger for greater success. The asshole takes it all in stride; he keeps his chin up and presses on.

#2. PUSH THE ENVELOPE.

While we tried to give as many examples in this book and cover as many topics as possible, there are countless areas in which to use the asshole approach to your advantage. Don't be afraid to take things to the next level, especially if you aren't getting the results you expected. If you have to, go to extremes. Take a drastic approach.

#3. PASS IT ON.

While it took some time, you finally came around to the asshole way of life. Now imagine if all this information was at your fingertips five or even ten years ago—your life would be incredibly different. Think of how this knowledge would benefit some of the people in your life—the brother that can't get ahead at work, the friend that sucks at dating, or the gym buddy that gets walked on more than the locker-room floor could all use come asshole advice. Pass on your knowledge. Be a mentor and teacher.

CHAPTER RECAP: You're an Asshole ... Now What?

Now what indeed. You've finished up your schooling and it's time to take on the world. As you head out there on your quest to be an asshole, remember the lessons you've learned from this book. Your success depends on it. Remember, an asshole is an asshole at all times. You must incorporate this new attitude into every aspect of your life. And don't forget to spread the wealth. Pass on the knowledge of Assholeology to anyone you think can benefit (and handle) its teachings.

Character Study

You: Yeah, we're talking about you. It's time for you to study yourself, see how you act, critique, and correct. As discussed in Chapter 3, it's important to track your progress so you can see how far you have come and how far you have to go. Keep notes. This way you can flip back to the appropriate lesson whenever you run into a roadblock. Being a successful asshole is now up to you. Make us proud.

Questions to Think About
- Come back to this question one week after being an asshole—how has your life changed?
- Come back to this question one month after being an asshole—how has your life changed?
- Come back to this question three months after being an asshole—how has your life changed?

What You *Should* Have Learned
- ❏ Don't listen to your critics.
- ❏ It's going to get shitty at times, but you have to roll with the punches.
- ❏ Don't be afraid to push the envelope.
- ❏ The asshole's journey never ends.
- ❏ You must continue to learn, evolve, and pass on your knowledge.

Part IV
A Guide to Recognizing Your Fellow Assholes

While Chapter 4 gave a few prime examples of typical assholes, this section will serve as a field guide of sorts to the everyday assholes you will run into. Learn about them and learn from them. Their ability to succeed in adopting the asshole attitude and using it to their advantage should educate and inspire. They pull it off. You can too.

The Political Asshole

DISTINGUISHABLE CHARACTERISTICS

A copy of *The Economist's* usually tucked under his arm by mid-morning as he heads out for a coffee (fair-trade only); his fingers are likely smudged with ink from the dailies he breezed through (*Times, Journal,* etc.) before dipping into the glossy. He's certain to have a pair of reading glasses on him even if his eyesight's a perfect 20/20. It helps him look well read and ready for a debate.

WHERE YOU'LL FIND HIM

Whether he's on the Hill or in City Hall, the Political Asshole is in the center of it all. However, he's most likely *not* the guy with his name on the door. No, the Political Asshole works his magic from behind the scenes as the mayor's, senator's, or even president's right-hand man. In that power position, he's able to be the muscle and the mind, and doesn't have to worry as much about his out-of-office activities as the elected official.

WHAT HE'S ALL ABOUT

Agendas—both his candidate's and his own. He has a lot to gain from working his angles besides bragging rights.

GREATEST ASSET

He can speak, extremely well. He's the perfect example of an ass-hole who knows what he's talking about. Like we've said, he's well read, but he's also able to deliver his well-informed thoughts in a clear and concise manner, leaving any opponent speechless.

> He's the perfect example of an asshole who knows what he's talking about.

WHAT HE CAN TEACH YOU

If you're going to speak your mind, make sure you're up to speed. The political landscape is ever changing so this guy's always sur-veying before he speaks. You should do the same, whether you want to discuss your party's stand on campaign finance reform or the form of your team's pitcher standing on the mound.

The Neighborhood Asshole

DISTINGUISHABLE CHARACTERISTICS

Rugged hands and ridiculous calves that have the ladies on your block swooning, earned from busting his ass with yard work and going for his morning jog. Both activities get him outside; visible to the housewives—and their husbands, who have to recognize him as the guy who's running shit in their 'hood. You on the other hand have been busy calculating potential fantasy points to see if a trade's worthwhile.

WHERE YOU'LL FIND HIM

6:30 A.M.: Headed out for his five-miler, waving to all the women on his route who time getting their newspapers with his run.

10:45 A.M.: Using your electric hedge clippers to shape his shrubbery. He didn't so much ask to borrow them as he told you he'd be using them.

12:15 P.M.: Greeting the mailman with a bottle of water, commiserating with him on how much working Saturdays sucks, and getting the lowdown on the crazy stuff that your neighbors get in the mail.

4:00 P.M.: Welcoming your girlfriend onto his patio. She brought him over a pitcher of sangria. *Wait a minute . . .*

WHAT HE'S ALL ABOUT

Remember in high school how there was the popular kid everyone knew and liked yet were intimidated by and sort of feared? Welcome back to high school pal. The Neighborhood Asshole is that popular kid. And unless you're him, it'd do you well to get in good with him.

GREATEST ASSET

Everyone likes him. Therefore no one would dare talk crap behind his back—let alone say something to his face. His visibility as the Neighborhood Asshole makes him the guy everyone wants at their BBQ. He's proof just how important it is to be liked. Not only does it keep your detractors quiet, it also scores you tons of invites.

WHAT HE CAN TEACH YOU

Get out there. Be seen. Be friendly. As an asshole, you want to build a rapport with everyone you see on a daily basis so if your attitude rubs them the wrong way one time, they're less likely to call you out. They can't be mad at you. You're *You*! You're not a d-bag. You're hilarious.

The Volunteer
Asshole

DISTINGUISHABLE CHARACTERISTICS

Sign-up sheets, petitions, pledge papers, pamphlets—he carries them all neat and organized in a clipboard as he works an angle with everyone he knows to get them signed up, donating, and volunteering. The Volunteer Asshole isn't just out there doing good, he's out there making you do good . . . and making himself look better in the process.

WHERE YOU'LL FIND HIM

Any type of community event that allows him to stand on a stage and grin. He might be doing it for free, but he looks money. And the exposure he gets at the countless neighborhood meetings, civic group functions, street fairs, save-the-park rallies, and pancake breakfasts helps him to get people eating out of the palm of his hand.

WHAT HE'S ALL ABOUT

Assholes can—and need—to be selfish. However, they need to balance out the selfishness by being selfless at times. So while his volunteering may be a little self-serving, the Volunteer Asshole is also truly giving back. Granted, it usually involves making others give back, but it's giving back nonetheless.

This guy knows how to work people.

GREATEST ASSET
Charm. This guy knows how to work people. And you can't get mad at him because he's working them for a good cause.

WHAT HE CAN TEACH YOU
Besides time management, the Volunteer Asshole is a good example of balancing self-interest with selflessness. True, you want to be an asshole for the benefits. But when you start only thinking of yourself, you've become a douche bag.

The Online Asshole

DISTINGUISHABLE CHARACTERISTICS

Over 1,000 Twitter followers, more Facebook friends than your city has people, and the latest smart phone in hand, on which he's checking websites you won't hear about for months.

He's telling you what to read, what to buy, and what sites to visit.

WHERE YOU'LL FIND HIM

Tweeting, 'Booking, and blogging—he's telling you what to read, what to buy, and what sites to visit. This guy was re-Tweeting the new must-watch viral video before you even accepted your first Friendster connection.

WHAT HE'S ALL ABOUT

He's completely wired and not afraid to let you know just how out of date you are. With the World Wide Web at his fingertips, he can correct anyone. Wrong stat. Wrong score. Wrong year. Everything he says, however, is right. And everything he does online will be the "right now" in about a year.

GREATEST ASSET

Knowing what's cool. Everyone looks to him when they want to know what they should be doing. He is the people's connection to what's in—and he knows it.

WHAT HE CAN TEACH YOU

Stay on the cutting edge. People will listen to you and come to you if you prove yourself. The Online Asshole has proven himself. Pretty soon, he won't even be the Online Asshole because he knows of something better than online.

The Coffee-Shop Asshole

DISTINGUISHABLE CHARACTERISTICS

He has a cup of coffee—not a latte, nor a cappuccino, nor a chai—next to his laptop and smart phone, but he's paying attention to neither because he's busy smirking at the barista and striking up casual conversations with the people around him. He looks important but approachable.

WHERE YOU'LL FIND HIM

Not going to answer that.

WHAT HE'S ALL ABOUT

Conversation and caffeine. There's plenty of room and coffee in his own home, but the Coffee-Shop Asshole chooses to bring his weekend work to the neighborhood shop. Why? Because it makes him look cool. No, not because he has a laptop. Because he's ignoring his laptop. Therefore that wink at the cute girl behind the bar or the quick recap of last night's game with the guy next to him carries more weight. He doesn't care about work. He cares about socializing. What a badass.

GREATEST ASSET
A carefree attitude. *What work?* The Coffee-Shop Asshole prefers to spend his time talking to you and sipping on this strong, caffeinated brew.

Work doesn't rule an asshole's life.

WHAT HE CAN TEACH YOU
Always seem busy, but never too busy to talk. Work doesn't rule an asshole's life. Living life is what he cares about. And if that can be shown off at a place where that serves a good cup of joe, more power to you.

The Asshole
Bartender

DISTINGUISHABLE CHARACTERISTICS

Skills at working bottles and glasses as well as people. The Asshole Bartender can pour and muddle your mojito before you can blink—or realize that you're laughing at his joke about what a pussy you are for ordering a mojito.

WHERE YOU'LL FIND HIM

Behind the bar.

WHAT HE'S ALL ABOUT

A good time. He doesn't go to the party. He is the party. People come and sit at his bar so they can get served a stiff drink and a good laugh. His ability to blur the lines of appropriateness with alcohol allows him to say what he really means, yet still receive a big tip.

GREATEST ASSET

A fast hand and a fast mouth. Not only does he serve up your Maker's Mark Manhattan quicker than you can count to three, he's holding multiple conversations with all of his patrons. The Asshole Bartender works fast. Before you realize he's poured you a second shot of Patrón, he's busy talking to your date about what she's doing after last call.

THE HOLE TRUTH

Check out how to be your own Asshole Bartender in Appendix A:
The Asshole Guide to Imbiding (page 153).

WHAT HE CAN TEACH YOU

You have to be quick. You need a quick hand, a quick mouth, and a quick wit. An asshole should be three steps ahead of everyone around him. And the only way to pull that off is by moving fast. The Asshole Bartender succeeds because he can move fast. Well, that and he can get people drunk.

The Gym
Asshole

DISTINGUISHABLE CHARACTERISTICS

Workout wear that doesn't *really* look like it's been worked out in.
The asshole's typically in shape, but it's hard to say how he pulls
this off. His gym time is usually spent socializing.

WHERE YOU'LL FIND HIM

In the gym, by the machines, near the benches, grabbing a mat,
filling up at the water fountain . . . but never actually working out.
He loves talking about working out. But it seems he never really
has the time—even though he's *at* the gym. Working a warehouse
full of attractive women takes up a lot of time.

WHAT HE'S ALL ABOUT

Fitness . . . we guess. Like we said, the Gym Asshole seems like
he's in shape, and certainly talks about it like he is—but it appears
he's more concerned with being at the gym than actually working
out in it. He's always chatting people up, giving workout tips, offering personal training sessions to the ladies as they leave spin class.
Yet he only breaks a sweat when the AC's broken.

GREATEST ASSET

Good genes? A healthy diet? An awesome metabolism? Something has to account for him being able to turn his workout time into social hour and not look like a fat slob.

Working a warehouse full of attractive women takes up a lot of time.

WHAT HE CAN TEACH YOU

Never let them see you sweat. Literally in this sense, but in more general terms, the Gym Asshole's ability to talk a good game without being called out on it is impressive.

The Asshole Dad

DISTINGUISHABLE CHARACTERISTICS

Usually has a kid in tow and has World's #1 Dad written all over him, without actually wearing a shirt or hat with that written on it. He's knowledgeable and encouraging enough to out-coach the coach during his son's soccer games, able to work his way into the reserved seating section for his little girl's big performance, and can make you feel like less of man and wish he'd adopt you at the same time.

WHERE YOU'LL FIND HIM

Sporting events, school plays, dance recitals, awards banquets—wherever proud parents congregate, he's there. And he's usually right up front, going on about how great his kids are.

WHAT HE'S ALL ABOUT

Competition—but not in the you-better-score-a-goal-today-or-you'll-be-walking-home way, in the my-kid's-*way*-better-than-your-kid way. Douche bags compete with kids. The Asshole Dad competes with other parents. Not only are his kids great, he is. He helps out at practice, builds sets for plays, and takes everyone for ice cream after the big win. He's the type of guy your kids wish you were.

GREATEST ASSET

Pride. He takes pride in his kids and isn't afraid to share it with anyone. Even if it does get nauseating, you can't complain because he's so involved. (And chances are, if he's this good, so are his kids.)

He's the type of guy your kids wish you were.

WHAT HE CAN TEACH YOU

Be proud of what you do and what've you made doing your wife. If you aren't the one talking about what you or your kids accomplished, you'll be listening to someone else talk about the same thing. And how f'ing annoying is that?

The Asshole Friend

DISTINGUISHABLE CHARACTERISTICS

Besides wearing your undying adoration on his sleeve, he's probably also wearing something he "borrowed" from you. Now that we mentioned it, doesn't that hoodie look familiar?

WHERE YOU'LL FIND HIM

Drinking your beer, driving your car, borrowing your lawn-mower—hell, he'd even be screwing your girlfriend if his wasn't hotter. You'd call any other person who acted this way a mooch. But he's too cool, and you want him to be your friend. You can't say no. Well maybe with the girlfriend thing . . .

People just like being around him.

WHAT HE'S ALL ABOUT

Reaping the benefits of having friends like you who'll go out of their way for him. You do everything for him, yet he holds the leverage over you. Why? He's cool. And you want to be seen hanging out with him.

GREATEST ASSET

Being a cool guy people want to hang with. He doesn't need an awesome television, or kegerator, or nice ride to get people to want to chill. People just like being around him.

WHAT HE CAN TEACH YOU

If you act cool, people will want to be your friend. Don't try too hard. That's not cool.

The Asshole Professor

DISTINGUISHABLE CHARACTERISTICS
Corduroy blazer with leather patches because it's so expected, it's hip. He's also probably balancing a stack of folders and books in one arm with a leather satchel slung over one shoulder (again, so expected, it's hip). He's a mildly disorganized authority figure—so cool.

WHERE YOU'LL FIND HIM
Walking through the campus, likely smoking a butt. He also frequents the bars where the upperclassmen do their weekday drinking. But he's never in the area on the weekends. He's got something going on in some other city.

WHAT HE'S ALL ABOUT
He makes you work for your grade. You want that A? Be ready to go above and beyond to get it. It's about substance with this guy, so don't think your usual tricks will work. He'll call you out and embarrass you in front of the whole class just because he can.

GREATEST ASSET

He's smart—both in the book-smart and worldly sense. You definitely can't bullshit this guy. Not only is he very well read, he seems like the type of teacher who's seen it all before (whether or not he has the years of experience).

You definitely can't bullshit this guy.

WHAT HE CAN TEACH YOU

Know your shit and don't be afraid to call out those who don't. That's basically how the Asshole Professor makes a living. As long as you have a handle on the subject, you're golden. Others can try to debate or find faults in your arguments, but as long as you've spent time studying and are confident, you can run shit.

The Party
Asshole

DISTINGUISHABLE CHARACTERISTICS

If you can even see him through the group of people crowded around at all times, you'll notice the Party Asshole probably has two drinks within reach (why waste time) and is in the middle of either telling a story, playing a game, or telling a story while playing a game.

WHERE YOU'LL FIND HIM

The heart of the party. He chooses to use his asshole attitude to be the center of attention. If beer pong's being played, he's on the table. If there's a card game going, he's dealing. If people are telling stories, he's the loudest. But nothing's ever forced. He was able to cut the beer pong wait list because no one would call him out on it; people want him to choose the next card game so he's in control of the deck; he's talking loud because the people in the back want to laugh along too.

WHAT HE'S ALL ABOUT

He's a born entertainer, which gives him leeway when it comes to being rude. It's not offensive; it's funny. Sure, the Party Asshole called your girlfriend a filthy slut when she hit the last cup, but he didn't *really* mean it.

He *is* the party.

GREATEST ASSET

He *is* the party. You've probably run into this before . . . you go to a party one weekend and it's okay, nothing special—there's plenty of booze and plenty of people, but it just seems to be lacking something. Then you go to a party at the same place, same booze, same people, and it's the most fun time you've had since you went wild in Amsterdam. What's the difference? The Party Asshole wasn't there the first time.

WHAT HE CAN TEACH YOU

Keep people entertained. Nobody likes to be bored. And the person who can keep things going will be remembered.

The Asshole Traveler

DISTINGUISHABLE CHARACTERISTICS
Besides an accent that really can't be placed—even though he's from Akron, Ohio—this guy runs out of room on his passport every two years. He's been everywhere. So if you think you're going to the next cool destination, guess again. He's already been there. And it was just okay. The place he's off to next is really where it's at.

WHERE YOU'LL FIND HIM
He was in Prague way before it was called the new Amsterdam and was over Krakow before you could find it on the map when you heard it was the new Prague. Good luck finding him now. But you'll definitely know him when you see him, likely in the airport.

WHAT HE'S ALL ABOUT
Traveling (*come on now . . .*). But beyond that, his thing is being one step ahead of you. Make that one step *way* ahead of you. This guy's obsessed with staying on the forefront of culture and prides himself on coming off as worldly. So much so, that he prefers to travel "with the people" via rail and budget airlines. He's in it for the real experience.

GREATEST ASSET

Being better than you. What? It's true. This guy excels at knowing what's cool, and he can bank on that. The Asshole Traveler also has tons of stories to tell over drinks, capturing the attention of the table, and leaving you there silent, stirring your mojito.

WHAT HE CAN TEACH YOU

An exciting story is important. When you talk, you want people to listen. So you better be talking about something that's worth listening to. Get out in the world and experience life. Granted, it might take you some time before you can predict the next "it" destination, but getting out of Akron might be a start.

The Nature Asshole

DISTINGUISHABLE CHARACTERISTICS
He smells like the woods. And being decked out in North Face and Patagonia, it looks as if he's ready to head there at any moment.

WHERE YOU'LL FIND HIM
The local farmer's market joking with the farmers about this week's crop of asparagus, or grabbing some gear at the outdoor supply store, or heading off for a weekend of hiking and kayaking as you get ready to watch *Anchorman* for the three-thousandth time.

WHAT HE'S ALL ABOUT
Living life. And letting you know how you're not. His eating right, staying in shape, and experiencing the beauty of watching the sunrise atop a mountain after a three-day trek really lets him lay it on thick when you talk about spending your Saturday with take-out, YouTube, and a thirty rack.

GREATEST ASSET
His health. Not just because he's going to live longer than you, but because he can hold it over you. What kind of comeback do you have if someone calls you unhealthy? None. You can try and

say his organic, un-processed food is crap. But have you tried it? Some of that shit is good. He has you beat here. And since it's a health issue and not just some healthy hating, your thick skin won't help much—especially if it's literally thick. (Dude, relax with the Twinkies.)

Get out there. Be active. Enjoy life.

WHAT HE CAN TEACH YOU

Get out there. Be active. Enjoy life. We realize this isn't some froofroo self-help book, but honestly, it'll work wonders. Just like you need to keep your mind sharp if you want to be a true asshole, you need to stay healthy. All right, enough with the motivational mumbo jumbo. Try not to be a fat slob.

The Yuppy Asshole

DISTINGUISHABLE CHARACTERISTICS

Nice clothes. Nice car. Nice watch. He's the guy you'd make fun of for looking so prissy if you didn't feel so inferior around him. How's a guy stay so put together? You could ask, but he'd probably just smirk and walk away. What an asshole.

He has no problem walking into these places like he owns them.

WHERE YOU'LL FIND HIM

The trendy bar downtown or in that new restaurant you're too intimidated to try. As you know, part of being an asshole is confidence, and this guy's got plenty. He has no problem walking into these places like he owns them. But what separates him from the other well-off douche bags inside is his class. He doesn't treat the employees like they're beneath him. He treats the other well-off douche bags that way.

WHAT HE'S ALL ABOUT
Enjoying life as a young professional. He feels on top of the world at this point and isn't afraid to let you know it. He works hard. He plays hard. And he couldn't care less what you think—unless you're going to affect his bottom line.

GREATEST ASSET
Confidence. You wouldn't know whether this guy just got promoted or laid off. He walks around with his head up and a satisfied grin on his face every day. Does he think he's better than you? Probably. Should he? Probably.

WHAT HE CAN TEACH YOU
Walk around like you own the place—even if you only have $27 in your bank account. Confidence is a state of mind, and lucky for you it's free. The better you feel about yourself, the better others will feel about you.

The Writer Asshole

DISTINGUISHABLE CHARACTERISTICS
Bloodshot eyes and the stench of a slow death.

WHERE YOU'LL FIND HIM
Starbucks or sleeping at his desk at his real job.

WHAT HE'S ALL ABOUT
Entertaining people. (Hopefully.)

GREATEST ASSET
For some reason, people *want* to read what he writes.

WHAT HE CAN TEACH YOU
In our case: How to be an asshole.

Appendix A
The Asshole Guide
to Imbibing

As discussed in Chapter 5: Act Like an Asshole (and touched on in just about every other section of this book), the Asshole knows how to make, serve, and hold down a drink. And he makes it look easy. Have you mastered that yet? To help you out—that's what we're here for—we've put together the essentials every aspiring A-hole needs to know when it comes to booze. Drink it in.

Pick Your Poison
Choose wisely.

Assholes know how to order the right mixed drink. It should be stiff and to the point. No whipped cream. No sugar rim. No tiny umbrellas. Your drink of choice says a lot about who you are. So you don't want it calling you out as a wimp or a douche bag. Keep the order simple—a vodka soda, a gin and tonic, a Jack and Coke. There's nothing more embarrassing than having to explain to the bartender the ratio of Midori to Blue Curaçao your drink requires.

Assholes know how to order the right mixed drink.

Choosing a signature cocktail is important. As discussed in the earlier chapters, tying a person to his drink of choice is a way to remember who he is (and it also works as a conversation starter). You want people to be able to do this with you and your drink.

And when it comes to actually drinking the drink, don't puss out or be obnoxious. You should be able to handle a straight shot of alcohol without a grimace. (If you can't, stick to beer.) But just because you are able to do it doesn't mean you should make a show out of it. Act like you've been to a bar before. Don't yell about taking shots, or how many shots you've taken, or how high the alcohol content is in the particular liquor you're drinking.

In terms of shots, the same rule applies as with a cocktail: Keep it simple. The idea is to enjoy the alcohol. If you want to diverge from a straight shot of whiskey or tequila, check out the recipes for the Three Wisemen and SoCo and Lime shots in this section.

Bottom line: You need to be able to pick your drink and handle your alcohol. Indulging without barfing or coming off as an obnoxious loser who cares more about the show of drinking than actually drinking is an absolute must.

Bar Etiquette
At the bar, you'll never see an Asshole do any of the following:*
(*These actions are total douche bag moves—see Chapter 1
for more on general douche-baggery.)

- Lean over the bar and wave his money at the bartender while yelling for his attention.
- Talk loudly on his cell phone about the crazy after-party he's going to.
- Push through the line at the bar because he really needs to order a round of Red Bulls and vodka for him and his "boys."
- Never buy a round.
- Keep his sunglasses on inside the bar.
- Leave a shitty tip.

Work and Play
Assholes know how to work the workplace mixer.

As discussed in Chapter 6, the Asshole has to keep a handle on himself around his coworkers. The people you work with should respect and fear you. This won't be the case if you pound too many shots at Friday's happy hour and start an impromptu karaoke session. You might as well not show up to work on Monday. While it's important to make your presence known at work events, be sure it's for the right reasons. When it comes to social events with coworkers, follow these two simple rules:

1. **Never get wasted.**
2. **Leave before it gets messy.**

Essential Cocktails

You can thank us when your bartending skills get you laid.

You'll notice that most of these recipes only call for a few ingredients. The simpler, the better. The point of drinking is to enjoy the alcohol. If you want a sugar high, bump a few Pixy Stix. The more adept you become behind the bar, the easier it will be to make small talk about what people are drinking, offer drink suggestions, and remember a person's usual cocktail (which, as we've been over, is a useful ability).

Contents

BLOODY MARY

2 OUNCES VODKA
1/2 CUP TOMATO JUICE
1½ TEASPOONS LEMON JUICE
TABASCO TO TASTE
WORCESTERSHIRE SAUCE TO TASTE
BLACK PEPPER TO TASTE
CELERY STALK
LIME WEDGE

Combine ingredients in a shaker (start with two dashes of Tabasco and Worcestershire and a pinch of pepper). Shake and pour into a tall glass filled with ice. Complete with the celery stalk and lime wedge. Taste and add additional Tabasco, Worcestershire, or pepper as desired.

ASSHOLE BARTENDER SAYS: Now this is the way to start the morning. Make yourself a Bloody Mary, cook up some eggs and bacon, and get rid of that hangover.

CAPE CODDER

1 OUNCE VODKA
CRANBERRY JUICE TO FILL

Fill a highball glass with ice. Pour in the vodka and fill with cranberry juice.

ASSHOLE BARTENDER SAYS: It's the perfect combination of alcohol and antioxidants (don't worry about what those are, just know that they're good for you).

THE 'HOLE TRUTH

Don't go too far when adopting the Cape Cod attitude. You're a pair of Nantucket red shorts and a madras belt away from becoming a douche bag.

COSMOPOLITAN

1 OUNCE VODKA
1/2 OUNCE TRIPLE SEC
1/2 OUNCE CRANBERRY JUICE
1/4 OUNCE LIME JUICE

Pour ingredients into a shaker half filled with ice. Shake well. Strain into a martini glass.

ASSHOLE BARTENDER SAYS: Serve this drink to get laid. Upgrade to premium vodka and cointreau instead of triple sec and it's a done deal.

GIBSON

1½ OUNCES DRY GIN
1/2 OUNCE VERMOUTH
3 PEARL ONIONS
LEMON TWIST

Shake gin and vermouth with ice in a shaker. Strain into a martini glass and garnish with onions and a lemon twist.

ASSHOLE BARTENDER SAYS: It's like a martini—except fewer douche bags order it. Subbing onions and a lemon twist for olives gives this drink a taste that's all its own.

THE QUOTABLE ASSHOLE
"I never drink anything stronger than gin before breakfast."
—W. C. Fields

GIMLET

2 OUNCES GIN
3/4 OUNCE LIME JUICE
LIME WEDGE

Shake gin and lime juice with ice in a shaker. Strain over ice in an old-fashioned glass and garnish with the lime wedge.

ASSHOLE BARTENDER SAYS: Don't let the lime juice fool you, the gimlet is a great gin-lover's drink. Play it cool the next time someone asks you to get them a gin and tonic and see if they want to try a gimlet instead.

GIN AND TONIC

2 OUNCES GIN
TONIC TO FILL
LIME WEDGE

Pour gin over ice in a highball glass. Fill with tonic. Garnish with a lime wedge.

ASSHOLE BARTENDER SAYS: Clean and simple—the gin and tonic should be your go-to cocktail whenever you want to feel refreshed.

IRISH COFFEE

1½ OUNCES IRISH WHISKEY
1/2 OUNCE IRISH CREAM
COFFEE TO FILL

Pour whiskey into coffee mug. Add coffee and top with Irish cream. Stir.

ASSHOLE BARTENDER SAYS: Your meal isn't complete until you've finished it with an Irish coffee and a good laugh. Not only will it sustain the buzz from your dinner drinks, it'll help energize you for the night ahead.

THE 'HOLE TRUTH

No milk. No sugar. No whipped topping. The cream liqueur does the job of all three.

LONG ISLAND ICED TEA

1/2 OUNCE VODKA
1/2 OUNCE LIGHT RUM
1/2 OUNCE TEQUILA
1/2 OUNCE TRIPLE SEC
1/2 OUNCE GIN
1 OUNCE SOUR MIX
SPLASH OF COLA

Pour all ingredients into a tall glass of ice. Stir.

ASSHOLE BARTENDER SAYS: Perfect for when you don't know what you want to drink—just that you know you want to get drunk.

MANHATTAN

2 OUNCES RYE WHISKEY
1/2 OUNCE SWEET VERMOUTH
2 DASHES BITTERS
1 CHERRY

Shake whiskey, vermouth, and bitters in a shaker. Strain into a cocktail glass. Garnish with a cherry.

ASSHOLE BARTENDER SAYS: The epitome of an asshole drink, the Manhattan mixes together the asshole's confidence (whiskey), likeability (vermouth), wit (bitters), and charm (cherry).

MARGARITA

1½ OUNCES AGED TEQUILA
1/2 OUNCE COINTREAU
1 OUNCE FRESHLY SQUEEZED LIME JUICE
1/2 OUNCE SIMPLE SYRUP
LIME WEDGE

Shake tequila, Cointreau, lime juice, and simple syrup in a shaker. Strain into a highball glass with ice. Garnish with the lime wedge.

ASSHOLE BARTENDER SAYS: It's not frozen and doesn't have a salted-rim; this version of the margarita just gives you what you want—tequila. Go dip a popsicle in a saltshaker if you're looking for the other stuff.

MARTINI

2 OUNCES GIN
1/8 OUNCE DRY VERMOUTH
2 LARGE GREEN OLIVES

Shake gin and vermouth in a shaker of ice. Strain into a martini glass. Garnish with the olives.

ASSHOLE BARTENDER SAYS: The straight-up gin martini is the way to go. (Much better than 007's vodka version—though his original Vesper (page 176) is pretty badass.)

ACCEPTABLE MARTINI VARIATIONS
- ☑ Dry
- ☑ Perfect
- ☑ Dirty
- ❏ Pink

OLD-FASHIONED

2 OUNCES RYE, BOURBON, OR WHISKEY
2 DASHES BITTERS
1 TABLESPOON OF SUGAR
1 CHERRY
1 ORANGE SLICE

In an old-fashioned glass with ice, muddle the sugar, cherry, orange, and bitters. Fill with ice then add the whiskey.

ASSHOLE BARTENDER SAYS: Don Draper drinks 'em. Enough said.

SCOTCH ON
THE ROCKS

2 OUNCES SCOTCH WHISKY

Pour Scotch over ice in an old-fashioned glass.

ASSHOLE BARTENDER SAYS: Why mess with a good thing?

THE QUOTABLE ASSHOLE
"I like my whisky old and my women young."—Errol Flynn

SCREWDRIVER

1½ OUNCES VODKA
2½ OUNCES ORANGE JUICE

Fill a tall glass with ice. Pour in orange juice. Pour in vodka. Stir.

ASSHOLE BARTENDER SAYS: If you're not a fan of tomato juice, the screwdriver is an acceptable morning-cocktail substitute. (Put down that mimosa.)

THE 'HOLE TRUTH

There's a fine line between the hair of the dog and day drinking. If you go out for brunch and stay for happy hour, chances are you crossed it.

SIDECAR

2 OUNCES BRANDY
½ OUNCE COINTREAU
1 OUNCE LEMON JUICE

Shake ingredients in a shaker. Strain into a cocktail glass.

ASSHOLE BARTENDER SAYS: A dark liquor drink, it's not as popular as gin and vodka cocktails, so it sounds more impressive when you ask for it at a bar. Just don't sound too smug. There's a fine line between an asshole who appreciates alcohol and a douche bag who tries too hard to be hip.

SOCO AND LIME

2 OUNCES OF SOUTHERN COMFORT
½ OUNCE LIME JUICE

Shake SoCo and lime juice in a shaker with ice. Pour into a large shot glass or shooter.

ASSHOLE BARTENDER SAYS: It's important for every at-home bartender to have a shot in his repertoire. And the SoCo and Lime is perfect because it's sweet enough for the girls and strong enough for the guys. (If the regular flavored whiskey isn't enough, you can always try the 100-proof variety.)

FOUL SHOTS

While the names are tempting, if you order one of the following, it's best to leave your manhood with the bartender.

- ☑ Fuzzy Navel
- ☑ Blowjob
- ☑ Sex on the Beach

THREE WISE MEN

½ OUNCE JACK DANIEL'S TENNESSEE WHISKEY
½ OUNCE JIM BEAM BOURBON WHISKEY
½ OUNCE JOHNNIE WALKER SCOTCH WHISKY

Shake and strain into a shot glass.

ASSHOLE BARTENDER SAYS: If you're looking to be gifted with some confidence, one or two of these shots might do the trick. Be able to handle your alcohol though. It's pretty embarrassing to make a face after taking a straight shot.

TOM COLLINS

1½ OUNCE GIN
2 OUNCES SWEET-AND-SOUR MIX
CLUB SODA

Fill Collins glass with ice. Add gin, sweet-and-sour mix, and club soda. Stir vigorously to work up a froth. Garnish with an orange slice and cherry (optional).

ASSHOLE BARTENDER SAYS: Serve to a gin-loving gal—they go down easy and she becomes even easier.

VESPER

**3 OUNCES GIN
1 OUNCE VODKA
½ OUNCE DRY VERMOUTH
LEMON TWIST**

Shake gin, vodka, and vermouth in a shaker with ice. Strain into a martini glass. Garnish with a lemon twist.

ASSHOLE BARTENDER SAYS: It's James Bond's original cocktail of choice, and a potent—but delicious—combination of gin and vodka. What more could you want?

VODKA TONIC

2 OUNCES VODKA
TONIC WATER TO FILL
LIME WEDGE

Pour vodka over ice in a highball glass. Fill with tonic. Garnish with lime wedge.

ASSHOLE BARTENDER SAYS: Captures the clean taste of vodka. If you want to impress your guests or lady friends, you better go top shelf. Using the kind that comes in a plastic handle and smells like rubbing alcohol will not have the same results.

VODKA WORTH TASTING
Next time you want to stir up a vodka tonic that'll go down smooth rather than come up quick, try one of these brands:
- ☑ Jean Marc
- ☑ Belvedere
- ☑ Chopin
- ☑ Ketel One
- ☑ Grey Goose

WHISKEY SOUR

2 OUNCES BOURBON OR WHISKEY
1 OUNCE LEMON JUICE
1 OUNCE SIMPLE SYRUP

Shake the ingredients with ice in a shaker. Strain over ice in a short glass.

ASSHOLE BARTENDER SAYS: It's not as ballsy as whiskey on the rocks, but the sugar and juice cut the cocktail in a way that makes it still pack a punch while not tasting like punch.

WHITE RUSSIAN

1 OUNCE VODKA
1 OUNCE COFFEE LIQUEUR
2 OUNCES MILK

Shake ingredients in a shaker. Pour into a short glass of ice.

ASSHOLE BARTENDER SAYS: It's like a milkshake for adults. And if it gets the Dude's seal of approval, it gets ours as well.

THE QUOTABLE ASSHOLE
"Hey, careful, man, there's a beverage here!"—The Dude, *The Big Lebowski*

Appendix B
The Asshole and the Hustle

Now that you've picked up the essential asshole skills to help you at work and with women, it's time to use the attitude to help fill your wallet. As you've learned, an asshole is convincing. He has a certain something about him—something you too can achieve—that allows him to persuade people. This power of persuasion is just what you need to start your own hustle.

An asshole is convincing.

What's a hustle?

We're glad you asked. A hustle is something you have happening on the side; it's not really legal or legitimate, but it can bring in some serious dough. Why doesn't everyone have a hustle then? Because everyone doesn't have *it*. *It* is what makes a hustler's hustle successful. Lucky for you, adopting the asshole persona will allow you to have *it*. So put *it* to good use. Try and make some money off one of these ventures. (Or at least have a good laugh thinking how crazy they'd be to try.)

Be a loan shark

Bad news: people are poor. Good news: you can take advantage of broke people by lending them money at a ridiculously high interest rate. You'll get in trouble if you threaten or harm your clients, but if you can resist the urge to break fingers if they don't pay you back, try it out. Start with a couple of your d-bag friends and see how it works for you.

Sell religious artifacts

Next time you're baking cookies or making a grilled cheese sandwich, put your artistic skills to the test and etch the image of Jesus, the

Virgin Mary, or another religious icon into the food. Post a photo of the object on eBay and you never know—you could end up making a fortune off a gullible religious fanatic.

"Discover" a mythic creature

Those Scottish fools have made a bundle selling pictures and footage of Nessy. And just recently, two guys down South "caught" Bigfoot and had his dead body to prove it.

Work a per diem job on company time

If you work in a profession where it's possible to get side jobs, use one of your paid sick days and work for someone else. Even if your temporary job only gets you a few bucks, factor in the time you're milking off the company clock and it usually proves to be worth your time.

Write letters from Santa

Odds are, you figured out there was no Santa the same way everyone else did: you noticed that Santa's handwriting was very similar to your mom's or dad's. Since typed letters don't suggest childlike Christmas innocence, offer to handwrite official Santa letter responses. Advertise your services near places where kids can sit on Santa's lap—most of those kids can't read, right?

Sell your friends' stuff

Next time a friend is moving or cleaning out her garage, offer to help—then keep your eyes peeled for stuff you can sell for profit. She may be planning on tossing out her recliner with the cigarette burn in the armrest, but maybe you can find a sucker on craigslist to buy it for $25. If you feel bad taking advantage of your friend, buy her lunch—just don't tell her why.

Trademark a buzzword

That d-bag Donald Trump actually had the balls to file a trademark request for the phrase "You're fired." So if you notice a term that's annoying enough to become this year's "That's hot," file an application. You could end up cashing in anytime someone uses your brilliant buzzword, though some people may have a few choice words for you.

THE 'HOLE TRUTH

We have dibs on "semantic mapping."

Start a dumping service

Telling your significant other that he or she is not so significant is a sucky task at best. Why not take on this messy chore for others? Sure, you'll end up consoling heartbroken men and women, but they don't have your number to drunk dial you in the middle of the night.

Hire out as a relationship assistant

Guys need as much help as they can get when it comes to keeping up with the women in their lives. Why not become the George to your friend's Jerry and help stay on top of him meeting his girlfriend's (or wife's) needs? You can keep her schedule straight for him, send flowers and chocolates on special occasions, and remember all those "little things" he always forgets. Just don't get found out—it could be the end of you both.

Turn tools into gentlemen

Think you have enough style and class to persuade some beer chugging frat guys to change their ways? Put together a plan and pitch it to them (and their girlfriends/mothers). With the popularity of shows like *Tool Academy*, there's definite interest in these male-Pygmalion transformations.

Perk up wallflowers

Some people just need a push to be social. Be the one who gives them that encouraging shove. Hire out as an advisor to shy guys and gals who want to take a more active role in life. Be careful though—once you release the beast, you might not be able to contain it.

Be a wingman for hire

When you're looking to score with an attractive member of the opposite sex, a wingman always helps. Market yourself as the ultimate wingman (including "testimonials" from previous "customers") and post an ad on craigslist or the entertainment section on your city's newspaper's website. Be ready to help out the socially inept, and possibly enlist the help of a hired target so that your efforts don't prove fruitless.

Become a creativity coach

Everyone has an idea for a book or a movie. If you're creatively inclined (and don't feel bad taking advantage of wannabe artists), post your profile on CreativityCoachingAssociation.com. As their own website states, CCCA "has not and cannot perform any verification of a coach's background or qualifications." Whaddya know? You're in.

Work as a life coach

One part personal assistant, one part therapist—100 percent bullshit. Yet thousands of people think they need a life coach. If you're an organized, somewhat sensitive person, help a brother out and coach him to improve his life. Odds are, if someone thinks they need a life coach, they probably do.

Act as a sex instructor

Most people want to be better in bed. Why not lead a class to help them do so? While you can't demonstrate the act, you can give tips to people to boost their confidence, in turn allowing them to cut loose more in bed. Be warned: you'll probably have to imagine your students doing the ol' bump and grind, which may or may not be a bad thing.

Start a March Madness pool

March is the one time of year when the whole country pays attention to college basketball. Consider your office—do most of them know more about *Top Chef* than college ball? Take advantage of their NCAA naiveté and start a pool—skimming an organizer's fee from the pool. Hey, you did have to use a ruler to make that grid so straight.

Start a death pool

Amy Winehouse. Your grandmother. Those guys from *Jackass*. Odds are, these people are not going to be around much longer. Why not work through your grief and make some money? Start an online death pool and allow users to place bets on the next person to kick the bucket. Keep a percentage of the profit, and get ready for the corpses to start piling up.

Sell wedding vows

These days, tons of women are ditching traditional vows and putting together their own personal take on "till death do us part." That leaves a lot of grooms with their thumbs up their asses. If you have writing credentials, submit your resume to wedding planners and event venues, offering you services as a "vow consultant." Charge per word and think of lots of ways to say, "I love you," without ever meeting the intended recipient.

While some of these may sound like harebrain schemes—and some really actually are—you have to remember, it's all about confidence. If you believe it, they'll believe it. And if they believe it, they'll pay you to do it. Taking money from a fool is so easy it should be illegal.

THE 'HOLE TRUTH

Actually, most of these side-operations are probably illegal. Therefore it's best to keep your hustle on the down low. No matter how good of an asshole you are, you can't beat the law.

FAQs: Frequent Asshole Questions

1. Why do I want to be an asshole?

Why not? Are things going so well right now? It's an experiment—like going vegan or not biting your nails. Except this book is a good idea. You should want to get ahead in life. This book, these ideals, will help you achieve that goal. Do you want to get ahead in life? (You shouldn't be thinking that question over.)

2. Is it okay for people to see me reading this book?

Yes. Don't be one of those douche bags that pretends to "accidentally" stumble onto a helpful book in the bookstore. Don't pretend you're just wandering aimlessly while you're really reading book titles out of the corner of your eye, constantly looking down the aisles for someone that might recognize you. And don't feel you need to buy this book along with three others so the cashier doesn't pay as much attention. It's okay: People can see you looking for it in the store. People can see you purchasing it. People can even see you reading it over a cup of overpriced coffee in that little bookstore café.

3. If I become an asshole and someone calls me an asshole, should I be offended?

No. You should hug them and say, "Thank you for noticing." Ask them what made them realize you were an asshole—and take notes. Ask what you could work on in the future and to rate you on how big of an asshole you were. Pick their jaw up from off the floor. This is great stuff.

4. Let's say I have this friend, Lee. He's a douche bag. Is it possible for me . . . I mean Lee . . . to take a step back and become an asshole?

It is possible. We have the technology. A douche bag is just an asshole that has gone too far. He is able to change as long as he's willing to reel back his d-bag tendencies and tone them down to a more tolerable asshole level. The first step is to recognize the douche bag moves and quit them cold turkey. (Stop picking on weak people. Stop being a follower. Stop spraying yourself with so much cologne.) We realize this is probably harder than it sounds. However, acknowledging that you have a problem is the first step. Now, you (or Lee) just have to put the asshole attitude in practice. Either do that or you'll get the shit kicked out of you. Both are acceptable outcomes.

5. Is it possible this approach just won't work?

It will always work if the person is willing to work for it. Becoming an asshole involves an open mind and a strong will. If it doesn't work, you don't have the moxie to put the plan in action. It happens. At least you gave it a shot. Now please wander over to the self-help section and pick up *Living with Mom in My Forties.*

6. I'm really bad with face-to-face confrontation; can all this be accomplished through other mediums like e-mail, text, and telephone?

Yes and no. You can communicate what needs to be said through the aforementioned technologies. But that's pussying out. And that's not how an asshole does it. Plus, it's much more fun in the flesh. It's an exhilarating feeling. Being an asshole to a person's face gets addicting. You'll want to do it all the time—to friends, coworkers, strangers, and your douche bag uncle at Thanksgiving dinner.

7. **Should asshole behavior be adapted according to geographic area? For example, an asshole in New York may reap the benefits of adopting the attitude, but an asshole in Alabama could get the tar kicked out of him.**

No, it's a one-plan-fits-all type of deal. Location doesn't matter. This works across the country—from the skyscrapers of New York to the rainy streets of Seattle. The asshole approach is universal.

8. **My girlfriend is taking advantage of me. Is it possible to change the situation by learning to be an asshole?**

Yes. Nothing is ever permanent. There are millions of lessons and approaches to learn from this book to see changes in your relationship in a matter of months, weeks, even days. Hell, you can change the path of your current relationship with a few simple steps right now. First, read this book cover to cover. Second, dump her ass. Last, find a better woman.

9. **How do I know when I'm around another asshole? Is there a handshake or gesture?**

Yes. There is an incredibly intricate scripted dance that every asshole must learn to become part of the tribe . . . Tool. Assholes just know their own kind. They recognize the characteristics of themselves in another person. Even though we are all friends, never approach another asshole. It's a silent brotherhood, kind of like all motorcycle riders or guys that watch HGTV.

Assholes just know their own kind.

10. If I'm an asshole, and don't like the change, is it possible to go back to my old self?

This isn't a sex change. It's not permanent. You can always go back to being a dickless pushover. Wow. Maybe there is a sex change involved. We stand corrected.

11. This book would be great for my dad. Is there an asshole age limit?

The asshole philosophy knows no age. A person can become an asshole at any point in his life. Even though he's older, Dad might still have a job to advance in or personal relationships to dominate. There are still mountains to climb even if parts of Dad's body don't exactly feel like a rock anymore. Now let's take a moment to stop thinking about Dad's erectile dysfunction, and move on to the next question . . .

12. How does becoming an asshole stack up against other "self-help" processes?

Every self-help theory is loosely based on the principles of being an asshole. They all teach the idea that you are the most important person and to do what's best for your personal well-being. Of course, most are based in mumbo jumbo that only clouds the thought process and dilutes the asshole philosophy. Forget that bullshit.

13. I've been peeing blood for the past week. What's that all about?

Wow. Wrong book my friend. We recommend something in the medical section of the bookstore or maybe seeing a fucking doctor. Good luck with that.

14. How quickly should I begin to incorporate these teachings?

Got something better to do? We recommend immediate action, but we'll cut you some slack and say to give it a shot as soon as you feel comfortable. Think of this book as a college text. Just don't buy it and then sell it back for beer money without ever opening it. Read. Reread. Take notes. Study. And unlike school, it's always encouraged to sneak a peek ahead.

15. I've got a newborn son. Is it too soon to start teaching him how to be an asshole?

A small child is like a sponge. It's never too soon to start planting the seeds. Think of teaching him the asshole way as you would a sport, or a different language, or any complex lesson that needs years to cultivate and mature. Start small with lessons on how to pick on the class bully, take what he deserves, and deal with his nagging mother (as soon as you figure that out).

16. Who the hell do you guys think you are?

Assholes. Thought that was obvious.

An Asshole
Abroad

In case you decide to become the Asshole Traveler, here's a list of translations for the word "asshole." You'll want to know when you're getting recognized.

Arabic
BAUSH

Czech
VOSEL

Dutch
KLOOTZAK

Finnish
PASKIAINEN

French
CONNARD

German
ARSCHLOCH

Greek
MALÁKAS

Hungarian
SEGGFEJ

Icelandic
FÍFL

Indonesian
BRENGSEK

Italian
STRONZO

Japanese
KUSOTTARE

Maltese
TOQBI

Mandarin
HÙNQIÚ

Norwegian
RASSHØL

Persian
KOSKESH

Polish
DUPEK

Portuguese
PENTELHO

Russian
MUDÁK

Serbian
SHUPAK

Slovak
KOKOT

Spanish
GILIPOLLAS

Swahil
M'KUNDU

Swedis
ARSLE

Urud
GANDH

INDEX

A

A-game, 96
"Am I Right?", 61
Antony, Mark, 18-19
Apologies, 32
Approaching a woman, 103-5
Asshole
    cares about the asshole most,
      30-31
    defined, 3-15
    detractor, 54
    essentials, 11-13
    evolution, 17-28
    examples, 6-9
    is always right, 31
    looking like an, 57-59
    reason for being an, 5-11
    talking like an, 60-61
    types, 45-55
    typical, 47
Athlete asshole, 49

B

Ball-brushing against her Brillo
    pad, 112
Bar, 86-89
    bartender, chummy with,
      86-87
    etiquette, 155
    games, 88-89
    names and drinks,
      remembering, 87
    peeing with others, 88
    talking to crowd, 88
Bartender, 86-87
    asshole, 133-34

Bed and befriend, 54
Birthdays and special occasions,
    94-95
Bloody Mary, 158
Bluntness, 39
Bonds, Barry, 10
Boss, 74-75
Bragging, 13
Breakups, 108-10
Bryant, Kobe, 9
Bullshit, people to never, 66
Buzzwords, 60
    trademark, 184

C

Calculated luck, 102, 112
Cape Codder, 159
Charlemagne, 19
Churchill, Winston, 21-22
Clothing
    style, 58
    tips, 58-59
Clown, being, 104
Coffee-shop asshole, 131-32
Cofriends, 72-73, 96
Confidence, 12-12, 101
Control, 32
Cosmopolitan, 160
CPR, 65
Creativity coach, 185
Current events, 63

D

Dad asshole, 137-38
Dating. *See* Opposite sex

About the Authors

Steven B. Green

Is an experienced actor/screenwriter/comedian, with several more slashes that shall remain nameless. He has appeared in musicals and plays off-Broadway, as well as in television shows and commercials. For many years, he performed with the Gotham City Improv Company in New York City. Currently, he performs stand-up in Los Angeles, improvisational comedy at the L.A. Connection, and teaches improv to kids and animals. Green lives at home in Los Angeles with his wife, three children, two dogs, and too many freaking cats. He realized during the writing process that he lost his asshole edge. So with the royalties from this book, he hopes to get back in touch with his asshole side and reclaim his place among the greatest assholes of our time.

Dennis LaValle

As one of Hollywood's top acting coaches, Dennis LaValle has dealt with his fair share of "not-ready-for-primetime" assholes. A graduate of New York University and now a transplanted Angelino, LaValle likes to think of himself as a bicoastal asshole in the best sense of the term. A classically trained actor, whose stage credits include numerous Shakespearean productions, he is, alas, best known as the goofy cowboy from the Pace Picante commercials. LaValle credits his beautiful wife Jeanne and their two kids for saving him from a life of meaningless sexual interludes ending in an alcohol-induced death face-down in the gutter.

Chris Illuminati

Is not really an asshole, he just acts like one every possible moment of the day. He fancies himself some type of authority and is a regular contributor to sites like AskMen.com, Asylum.com, and TheBachelorGuy.com. He writes about relationships, careers, and sex. He lives in New Jersey with his wife and cat Stephen. Yes, that is his real last name.